SMALL-SPACE
VEGETABLE
GARDENS

SMALL-SPACE
VEGETABLE
GARDENS

Growing Great Edibles in Containers, Raised Beds, and Small Plots

ANDREA BELLAMY

TIMBER PRESS
PORTLAND, OREGON

To my daughter, Lila,
and future gardeners everywhere.

Front cover photos by Jackie Connelly (upper right and lower left) and Steve Masley (lower right).

Frontispiece: Teeming with herbs and vegetables, this small backyard oasis is a wonderful example of edible landscaping.

Illustrations by Jen Wick
Photo credits appear on page 205

Second printing 2015

Published in 2014 by Timber Press, Inc.

The Haseltine Building
133 S.W. Second Avenue, Suite 450
Portland, Oregon 97204-3527
timberpress.com

Printed in China
Text design by Susan Applegate
Cover design by Jen Wick

Library of Congress Cataloging-in-Publication Data

Bellamy, Andrea.
   Small-space vegetable gardens: growing great edibles in containers, raised beds, and small plots/Andrea Bellamy.— First edition.
      pages cm
   Other title: Growing great edibles in containers, raised beds, and small plots
   Includes bibliographical references and index.
   ISBN 978-1-60469-547-2
   1. Vegetable gardening. 2. Farms, Small. I. Title. II. Title: Growing great edibles in containers, raised beds, and small plots.
   SB321.B38 2014
   635—dc23   2014009485

A catalog record for this book is also available from the British Library.

Contents

Preface

All around us, a movement is taking place. People are rigging up window boxes for growing herbs, making room on the fire escape for a pot of tomatoes, renovating neglected flower beds to make way for raspberries and rhubarb, and convincing landlords to turn over a few square feet of lawn for food production. Families are joining waitlists for community garden plots, signing up for canning workshops, and getting to know their local growers at the farmers' market.

The economy, self-sufficiency, sustainability, taste, health—whatever your reasons, it is always a good time to grow your own organic food. And you can do it, no matter how small your gardening space.

I grow food for all these reasons, but most of all I do it because it feels great. I love working outside and getting my hands dirty. I love connecting with other gardeners and sharing seeds and ideas. And I love harvesting something I have grown and eating it fresh that night for dinner. Yes, it is local food— really local food. But mainly it's just good food.

For me, gardening has been a lifelong obsession and an experiment in trial and error. Lots of error.

And, believe it or not, that is something I love about growing food—it keeps me on my toes. Just when I think I've finally mastered this urban farming thing, nature proves me wrong. The key, I think, is to pay attention—to celebrate each perfect potato, learn from mistakes, and, above all, enjoy the process.

This book walks you through the basics—and then some—of planning, creating, and tending an organic food garden in a small space. This is the book I wish I'd had when I was a new gardener, and I hope it will be a helpful resource and an inspiration to you. Most of all, I hope you get hooked on gardening and growing your own good food.

◀ This tiny garden supplies everything from herbs to vegetables to fruit.

Finding Space

Not all that long ago, vegetable gardens were relegated to the backyard. Tucked away from the eyes of neighbors and visitors, the veggie patch was often plain and utilitarian. It served one function: to feed the family.

Now, edibles are everywhere—even on the grounds of the White House. And not only gardeners are doing the growing. Foodies are discovering the fresh flavors of homegrown produce and herbs. Self-sufficient types are learning how to feed themselves—from seed to plate. Many of us are trying to lighten our carbon footprint and save money by eating closer to home. Finally, the veggie patch is having its day.

As popular as growing our own food has become, few people have a spare 200 square feet for a vegetable garden. What you may have, however—or have access to—is a balcony, a patio, a plot in a community garden, or even a small yard. Happily, that's all you need to create a bounty of edibles that can bring sustenance and personal satisfaction.

But first: Where to get growing?

◄ Gardens can happen in the most unexpected places.

Thinking Outside the Plot

Almost everyone has access to more space than they realize. It just takes a little creative thinking to see it. I didn't have the space to grow both peas and beans inside the confines of my patio, for example, so I co-opted the back side of my fence, which separates my patio from an alley. In only a narrow strip of soil at the base of the fence, I planted a family of pole beans, which climb up twine attached to the fence.

Take a look at your back alley: Could you install narrow raised beds along the alley's edge? Take a look at your sidewalk: Could you grow food in the space between it and the street? Take a look at any hard outdoor surfaces: Could you have a container garden on your driveway, porch, fire escape, or staircase? Take a look at your rooftop: Is it flat and relatively easy to access? (Remember that you will have to get pots, soil, and water up there, too.) Could it support the weight of a container garden? Take a look at the land surrounding your building: Could you convince your landlord or homeowners association to let you start a garden?

Container Gardens

When gardening on a rooftop, balcony, or other similar place lacking in soil, containers may be your only option. Or perhaps you just like the visual impact or control offered by gardening in pots. Luckily, you can find a nearly endless variety of container styles—from rustic to modern and everything in between. And with a large enough container, you can grow almost anything in a pot—even fruit trees.

This narrow alley bed is home to espaliered fruit trees, garlic, corn, potatoes, rhubarb, and a worm bin.

PROS Visual impact provided by colorful or unique containers. You can also provide perfect soil, move pots around, create a garden where there isn't one, reduce soil compaction, and control pests and weeds.

CONS Pots can dry out quickly or become waterlogged if drainage is insufficient. Nutrients must be replaced frequently. Plants can become root-bound if pot is too small.

Community Gardens

The classic solution to the space-shortage problem, community gardens have been around in various forms for centuries. Whether gardened communally or clearly divided into individual plots, community gardens—and their British counterpart, allotment gardens—can be great places to get growing. In addition to paying an annual plot fee, gardeners are usually expected to help maintain the overall health of the garden by doing basic garden tasks (such as weeding the common areas or maintaining the compost bin) or by contributing their time through fundraising or other administrative tasks. In exchange, you'll typically get a plot of your own, along with access to the tools to maintain it.

PROS Meeting your neighbors, learning from more experienced gardeners, and sharing resources—often including water, compost, and garden tools. Usually, the cost for an allotment or plot is reasonable, or even waived for those with lower incomes.

CONS You may have to wait a while to get a space; waiting lists can be long. If the garden is far from your home, it can be inconvenient to maintain and harvest. Theft can also be an issue.

Shared Backyards

Cities are full of underutilized space, much of which is on private residential property. You may have walked by lawn after empty slate of lawn and imagined what you could grow if some of it were yours.

If you have no garden space of your own, consider a shared yard. Nearby friends or relatives might be willing to let you garden on a corner of their property. Another

'Fortex' pole beans grow up a sunny exterior panel of my fence.

alternative, Sharing Backyards (sharingbackyards.com), matches people looking for garden space with those willing to share. You can also try posting a note on a community forum or other online forum, doing it the old-fashioned way and posting a note on a bulletin board at your local coffee shop or community center, or even knocking on doors of neighbors who might have space to spare. It's all about connecting with your community.

Some people may want to charge a small fee for the use of their space, while many are just happy to have their yard beautified for little effort on their part. Most property owners would be grateful for a share of the produce.

Key to this arrangement is making sure to keep your plot tidy and being respectful of the property owner's tools, utilities, and space.

PROS Meeting your neighbors, making a friend or two, and gaining access to garden space.

CONS Can take a lot of legwork to find the right space and property owner to share with. Can be unstable—the property could be sold or leased to new renters who are not into sharing, or the property owner could decide that the situation isn't working halfway through your growing season.

Community gardens are an old idea enjoying new popularity.

◄ Vertical container growing makes this balcony welcoming and productive.

Parking Strip Garden

In many neighborhoods, there's a sizable grassy strip between sidewalk and street. While it can be a challenging place to garden (it's not known as the "hellstrip" for nothing), if you've got a fairly wide boulevard and a not-too-busy street, this often-overlooked space could be your ticket to fresh produce.

PROS Curb appeal, enhances space for visitors and neighborhood, and utilizes nearby, inground gardening space.

CONS Compacted soil, pollution from vehicle traffic, and damaged plants due to careless passersby. Theft can be an issue. (Also: dogs. Enough said).

Gardening at Work

Forward-thinking employers offer wellness benefits to employees. A workplace garden supports a healthy lifestyle and provides opportunities for workers to be physically active, connect with coworkers, and relieve stress—all valuable advantages for employers. Plus, workplace gardens make the company look good from sustainability and community engagement perspectives—key selling features if you decide to approach your boss about a garden project.

Before asking your employer about creating a garden, think about whether you want to take over an existing garden space for your personal use or create a multiple-user garden—a community garden for the workplace. Also determine how and where the garden will be constructed, who will maintain it, and on whose time this maintenance will occur.

PROS Having fun at work, using your lunch break to de-stress, and gardening where you spend a good chunk of your week. Your company might even agree to pay for construction materials.

Turn the space between street and sidewalk into a vegetable plot.

CONS Getting the go-ahead could take ages in large or bureaucratic organizations. The soil may be of questionable quality—potentially compacted and polluted with industrial wastes. Coworkers may lose enthusiasm after their initial interest, leaving you to maintain the garden.

Gardening at School

School gardens have a long history. They have been used to teach young people about healthy lifestyles, environmental stewardship, and nutrition, and they help students connect with and build community.

PROS Connecting with and learning from students and parents, and improving the biodiversity and sustainability of your campus or schoolyard.

CONS The approval process can be painfully slow. You will probably have to raise funds or get materials donated to build the garden.

Gardening for parents

Many elementary school garden programs involve parents. This is a great way to get into gardening and learn with your child. If your child's school does not have an existing garden, approach the principal and volunteer to lead the project.

Gardening for high school and college students

A rising number of high schools and universities have areas dedicated to community garden–style growing. If your school doesn't, approach your student council or ask your favorite teacher to work with you to get one approved and built. In college, your student association is a good place to start, as are faculty members who teach environmental and social sciences.

School gardens educate and engage on many levels.

Assessing Your Space

Although we can meticulously plan a planting scheme, short of leveling trees or neighboring buildings, we can't do much about the sunlight our gardens receive.

External factors have a huge influence on the success of a garden; take the time to observe the things that impact your space before leaping in and planting. Don't despair if, at first glance, your potential location seems unsuited to growing food. Think creatively: the problem is often the solution. Working with what is already available on your site will always be more satisfying and will yield better results than fighting natural conditions.

◄ Gardening success is all about making the most of what you've got.

When sizing up your space, considering a few external factors can help you design the healthiest, most productive garden possible.

Climate

Where you live determines your garden's climate, the length of the growing season, and how much rainfall you receive—all of which affect what you grow and how you grow it. Some edibles simply grow better in some regions than they do in others. Recognize the characteristics of your climate, and consider how they will impact what you can grow.

For example, drought-tolerant rosemary, a Mediterranean native, needs dry, warm summers to thrive. That doesn't mean it can't be grown in rainy, mild climates, but you should try to create conditions that resemble rosemary's native habitat: provide excellent drainage by amending the soil with sand or perlite, and plant it in the sunniest spot in the garden.

Your area's hardiness zone is another important consideration. Every city or region is assigned a zone number based on its lowest average annual temperature—from Fairbanks, Alaska (zone 1) to Mazatlán, Mexico (zone 11). Plants are also given a zone rating, which offers gardeners a hint as to whether that type of plant will survive the winter in their area. For example, if you live in Halifax, Nova Scotia, zone 6, you should look for plants that are hardy (frost-tolerant) to zone 6 or lower.

The trouble with zone ratings, however, is that a plant's ability to thrive in a certain location depends on more than just minimum temperatures—rainfall and soil conditions, for example, also play big roles in hardiness, as do summer heat levels. Plants grown in containers are also less cold tolerant than their inground counterparts—something else to consider when choosing what and where to grow. You can find out which zone you live in by searching online for "plant hardiness zones" and "plant heat zones."

All that said, hardiness zones don't even come into play as far as annual edibles are concerned—most of these plants will not survive the winter anyway. But zones are definitely an important factor when you're growing plants such as fruit trees or perennial herbs.

A microclimate is an area in which the climate differs from the larger area around it. Hotter, cooler, wetter, or drier—a microclimate can be as small as a balcony or as

Most apple varieties are hardy to zone 4, but that doesn't mean they're easy to grow in every hardiness zone higher than that. They also have a chilling requirement—a certain number of hours below 45°F—that allows them to enter dormancy.

large as a valley. Many factors can change the microclimates of your garden: light bouncing off a patio or wall, heat radiating from a metal fire escape, a wind tunnel created between buildings, or a clothes dryer that vents onto your balcony. Pay attention to these factors and, if you can, use them to your advantage.

To Everything There is a (Growing) Season

The growing season refers to the length of time between your area's last killing frost in winter or spring and the first killing frost in autumn or winter—in short, it describes the season during which plants grow. Government organizations such as the U.S. National Climatic Data Center or Environment Canada track these dates and make them available online (search "average frost dates" or "growing season length").

The length of your growing season will help determine what you can plant, since some plants—melons, for example—require a long, hot growing season. Seed packets often provide the number of days required for a seed to grow into a harvestable vegetable (known as days to maturity). If that number exceeds the number of days in your growing season, you should start your seeds indoors ahead of your last frost date and transplant them outside after the weather has warmed, protect the plants from late-season frosts until they can be harvested, or choose a variety that is quicker to mature.

Light and Shade

Sunlight—or lack of it—is a huge factor in a garden. Most fruits and vegetables require upward of six hours of direct sunlight daily to thrive. A sunny balcony or garden is considered ideal (you can always create shade if you or your plants are baking), but any patio that receives some sunlight in summer can produce food.

Make a point of recording how many hours of direct sunlight your site receives and where it falls. Then work with the amount of light you have. Fruiting vegetables such as tomatoes and cucumbers will be happiest in your sunniest spot, while root vegetables can get by with a little

Fruiting vegetables such as cucumbers, tomatoes, peppers, eggplants, and squash prefer eight or more hours of direct sunlight a day.

less than full sun, and leafy greens are fairly forgiving of part-shade conditions. If you really are in the dark, grow mushrooms.

I've had great success growing a salad garden in an area that receives about three hours of sunlight daily in spring, and perhaps four in summer. For most months of the year, it produces tender butter lettuces, peppery arugula, mild mizuna, and a number of other greens, plus radishes, chervil, and even snack-sized carrots. Even with limited sunlight, it's wildly productive.

There are a few things you can do to increase the amount of light your crops receive, even without limbing nearby trees (though, if you can do that, it'll help). If the exterior walls of your home are white, remember that sunlight will bounce off the surface, providing additional light (and heat). You can mimic this effect by setting up a reflective panel such as a mirror or foil-covered board (or mitigate it using a dark color). You can also use reflective mulches: silver or red foils that cover the soil surface and reflect light up into the plant's leaves. As an added benefit, reflective mulches also increase soil temperature and block weeds.

In addition to limiting your plant choices, shady gardens come with another set of problems: an increased susceptibility to pests and diseases. Some diseases, such as mildew, thrive in damp shade. Insect pests such as slugs and snails are happiest there, too.

Edibles for Part Shade

An area receiving approximately four hours of sunshine daily is in part shade. The conventional wisdom is that, in these conditions, you can rule out heat-loving fruiting vegetables such as zucchinis, tomatoes, melons, and peppers, while leafy greens and berries will thrive. But in my experience, many edibles that prefer full sun—even fruiting vegetables—often produce in part shade. They just don't produce as much. So if you've got your heart set on tomatoes, give them a shot. Experimenting is half the fun, anyway. Increase your odds of success by choosing the following shade-tolerant edibles:

alpine strawberries	chard	lemon balm	parsley
arugula	Chinese cabbage	lettuce	peas
Asian greens	chives	mesclun greens	radishes
beets	cilantro	mint	rutabagas
blackberries	currants	mizuna	scallions
blueberries	gooseberries	mushrooms	sorrel
bok choy	kale	mustard greens	spinach
carrots	komatsuna	oregano	tatsoi

Blueberries are a good choice for partial shade conditions—areas that receive four hours of sunshine daily.

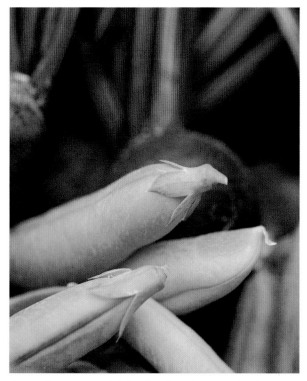

Peas and beets are good choices for a less-than-sunny locale.

Herbs such as thyme and basil prefer full sun and well-drained soil.

Size

Small-space gardening means different things to different people: it could mean a 4-by-8-ft. raised bed in a community garden, or a tiny window box. Obviously, the size of your site impacts what you can grow; some edibles just aren't practical in a tiny garden. For those of us who want to grow *everything*, this can be a tough lesson to learn. This book will help you decide what to plant in your small space, and share small-space growing techniques like using cut-and-come-again crops and vertical gardening. And if your balcony gets truly full, you can always look for additional garden spaces.

Even the smallest corner of a yard can be productive, especially with reflective heat from bricks or concrete.

Soil

Soil is arguably the single most important element of any garden, regardless of the plot's size. But to succeed, small-space vegetable gardens are especially dependent on good soil quality. Whether you're growing food in the ground, in containers, or in raised beds, you can assess your existing soil and improve it if necessary, using the techniques discussed in this book.

Water

Along with soil and sun, water makes your garden grow. Or not. Because poor drainage is death to plants, identify whether your site might have pockets where water will pool. (Cold air will also hang out in low-lying areas, creating frost-prone microclimates.)

Your garden should be within easy reach of a hose or tap. Balconies are often lacking in water access, and lugging a watering can from your kitchen sink every day can be a royal pain. Consider installing a rain barrel that catches and stores rainfall to reduce your trips to the tap (and the impact on storm sewers).

Wind

Wind can be a big factor in the city, especially on rooftops and balconies. Heavy winds speed moisture loss from the soil, knock over containers, and shred delicate leaves. Mulching reduces soil moisture loss, and windbreaks provide shelter for tender vegetables. A fence or trellis covered in edible climbers such as runner beans or blackberries makes a great windbreak. Grouping containers together will help keep them from toppling over.

Weight

If you garden on a balcony or rooftop, weight is an important consideration. Containers, soil, plants, water, and

Gardens on balconies and rooftops require considering water ▸ (how far), wind (how prevalent), and weight (how much).

people add up to a heavy load. Consult with your landlord or an engineer or builder on weight restrictions to ensure that your balcony is up to the task.

You can reduce the load by choosing lightweight containers such as plastic, resin, or fiberglass. Use the light and airy soil specifically designed for container growing. Take the weight off the floor with wall- and railing-hanging planters and hanging baskets.

Hanging baskets are a great way to gain extra gardening space—and they keep the weight load down on balconies.

Pollution

You are growing food to eat, and you want healthy, organic edibles. But if your efforts are undermined by pollution, you may be inadvertently consuming contaminants. Fortunately, you can usually lessen pollution's effect on your plants by making sure your soil is healthy and free of toxins.

Before you begin working an inground plot, check to determine what was on your land before you were. Could it have been a gas station? A tannery? A dry cleaner? Chemical contaminants from industrial businesses can devastate the soil for generations.

If you are in doubt about this aspect of your soil, build raised beds using new soil, or, if you're set on gardening in the ground, get your soil tested before you plant.

Do not grow edibles near patios or beds built with treated lumber: its chemical preservatives leach into surrounding soil. Also avoid growing food next to busy streets; along with the vehicles' exhaust, cars tend to cloak plants with a film of grit. If the only space you've got is street-side, grow root vegetables to avoid most of the grime.

Pests

At some point as a gardener, you will curse a pest for a) peeing in your garden, b) digging up your seedlings, or c) wolfing down your almost-ready-to-pick produce. So when designing your garden, you would be smart to look at your space with an eye for potential troublemakers.

It is difficult to predict which types of insect pests your garden will attract. But unless you're gardening on a high-rise balcony, urban gardeners can count on visits from raccoons, squirrels, rats, cats, or dogs. In suburban and rural areas, deer, rabbits, and groundhogs join the fun. Finally, consider the human pest. Native to both country and city, they often have little respect for gardens. If yours is exposed to the public, you can probably expect litter, crushed or broken plants, and theft.

If your soil has a sordid past, build up. Raised beds keep your crops off the ground.

Dissuade larger pests such as cats from digging in newly cultivated beds by covering beds with chicken wire or by keeping exposed soil frequently watered—cats seem to prefer digging in dry beds.

If deer or dogs are an issue, consider a fence to keep them at bay. Line the bottom of raised beds with hardware cloth to deter burrowing animals such as moles and groundhogs. In high-traffic locations, a low fence can define your space and prevent people from stepping on your plants.

Proximity

You may not have much of a choice where your garden is located, but situating it as close as possible to where you conduct your daily activities, especially cooking, is always a good idea. Consider how you move through and interact with your space, and lay out your garden appropriately. For example, if you walk down your front steps and across your front lawn to the sidewalk every day, perhaps the best place for your crops is along this route. You will be more aware of how your garden is faring and more likely to tend to it if you see it several times daily.

A front yard doesn't have to be just for show.

By adding an edible garden in front, this home increased its curb appeal—and its usefulness.

Design in a Small Area

Designing a small garden comes down to a lot of tough choices. Rarely is there room for everything you want to include, so you have to do a bit of soul searching to make decisions about what is really important. Do you want to make a dedicated effort to grow as much of your own produce as possible? Or do you want to grow only a few herbs to support your cooking habit? What else needs to happen in your growing space besides growing? Would you sacrifice a barbecue for a couple of blueberry bushes? The desired scale of food production will have a huge impact on how your garden will look.

◄ Gardeners must balance multiple demands in a small outdoor space. Through careful planning, this gardener produces a lot of food on a modest patio.

For me, gardening is a balancing act. I aim to grow as much food as I can in my small space, while still allowing room for things other than plants—a barbecue, a place to eat, even a corner where my daughter can splash in a wading pool. Style-wise, I am a contradiction, loving the clean, modern lines of minimalism, yet coveting the sensory overload of an abundant veggie plot. I am lucky because I have both a balcony and a community garden plot, and therein lies my personal solution: keep it neat and restrained at home, and go wild off site.

As much as I sometimes covet a big backyard, I know that blessings come with a small garden. It forces you to be organized, because you have no place to hide general garden junk. Small gardens are also manageable. No need to spend hours fussing over . . . well, anything—unless you want to. Gardens can take a lot of work, so it can be best to start small no matter how big your garden space. Forget the yard envy, and focus all your efforts on making your little space as beautiful and productive as possible.

Finding Your Personal Style

Deciding how you want your garden to look can be a difficult task. You might find yourself drawing a blank—or having differing visions of your personal paradise.

Take a moment to disregard the reality of your space. Forget its limitations. Let your mind wander and think about your dream garden. What do you imagine? It could be the charming, formal kitchen garden at a bed and breakfast you visited in France. It could be your grandfather's sun-drenched veggie patch behind the old house, or the casual luxury of the penthouse deck you can see from your balcony.

Finding and embracing these inspirations will set the theme, or mood, of your garden. And although you might not be able to duplicate your dream garden at home, you can use its characteristics to influence even a small garden design.

You may not have room for a traditional kitchen garden, for example, but you can incorporate some of its elements

Maybe all you want to commit to—or have room for—is a rooftop garden of fresh vegetables.

into any space. Your choice of plants and structures will all hint at your garden's character. Keeping the essence of your dream garden in mind will help you stay on track as you choose containers and make other design decisions.

Inspiration is Everywhere

Check out garden books and magazines; garden, home design, and style blogs; and online photo galleries such as Flickr.

You may want to borrow a technique used by interior decorators, fashion designers, and creative types from all fields and create a mood board. This is a collection of images, objects, text, and textures that inspire you and provide a visual sense of your garden ideas. Arrange these elements on poster board, in a notebook, or on a site like Pinterest. This will help clarify your style preference and provide direction for a clear final vision. Other sources of inspiration may include:

- **Your home.** The mood of a favorite room can be recreated in your outdoor space.

- **Your travels.** A favorite vacation spot can be your muse.

- **Your neighbors' gardens.** Peek over fences and check out what's growing in your neighbors' yards to learn what grows well in your area.

- **Memory.** The gardens of childhood often leave lasting impressions; capture the magic in your own space.

- **Local garden centers and botanical gardens.** These organizations often have drool-inducing displays and ideas you can borrow.

Potager is a French term for an ornamental vegetable garden. Herbs and flowers are often included.

Design for Year-Round Interest

All gardens naturally have peaks and valleys. There are the obvious seasonal changes: the abundance of summer giving way to cooler temperatures and reduced production, winter dormancy, and finally, spring rebirth. But there are also the mini-cycles that occur within a single growing season: containers or beds that are suddenly—glaringly—empty after a harvest, or greens that, seemingly overnight, have bolted (produced seeds rather than the leaves or roots we harvest) and are now flopping onto your pathways. These cyclical lows may not be the prettiest times in the garden, but with a bit of planning, they don't have to be unsightly.

Define the structure

When designing a garden, professionals usually start with what they call the hardscape: non-plant materials in a garden. Pathways, patios, raised beds, stone walls—these are the structures that will define your space (and, in areas where winter kills off all but the hardiest specimens, help your garden hold its shape, and interest, all year long). Even when your crops have died back or are buried under snow, the lines of a well-designed garden are still evident; if yours looks decent even without plants, you've done well. In a balcony or patio garden, this might mean choosing bold containers, or placing them in a way that emphasizes balance and pattern. In a small yard, this could mean building raised beds bisected by a well-defined pathway, or adding a striking feature such as a sculpture or other piece of art.

Add trees and shrubs

If you have room for a small tree, add one or more. If you have room for berry shrubs, add two or three. These beauties offer more than just summer or fall fruits: even deciduous trees and shrubs will provide structure and year-round interest. Fruit trees also show off spring flowers, while blueberries have brilliant fall color. Also consider perennial herbs such as oregano, thyme, and rosemary for their evergreen status, and hardy favorites such as kale and Brussels sprouts for winter interest.

Succession plant

Succession planting, a technique that produces a series of crops from a single plot or container, is most often thought of as a way to get the most out of a small garden, but it has uses beyond increased productivity. By immediately replacing harvested edibles with new seedlings (or popping a seed into a hole left by a vacating

A fond recollection of a favorite canoe trip may have inspired this unusual vegetable garden.

Vegetables thrive alongside flowers in this contemporary outdoor room.

vegetable), you can limit the number of empty spaces in your garden.

Plant wisely, harvest wisely

Choose crops that do not leave your bed or container empty when harvested. For example, plant loose-leaf lettuce—which can be harvested by removing a few outer leaves at a time—rather than head lettuce, which is harvested by removing the entire plant.

Consider color, texture, shape, and form

There's no reason a vegetable garden has to be a nondescript sea of green. Consider repetition, balance, and contrast in your planting plan. Choose colorful edibles such as bright rhubarb, scarlet runner beans, jewel-toned cabbages, purple bush beans, yellow tomatoes, or pink eggplants. Aim for a variety of leaf shapes and textures—contrast crinkly leafed chard with ferny carrot tops, and large-leaved squashes with the tall, slim straps of leeks.

This garden's well-defined beds, while asymmetrical, feel neat and orderly.

Remember the "thriller, filler, spiller" axiom when planting a container

Garden writer Steve Silk coined this phrase to describe various plant qualities. A thriller is a showstopper plant you can build a container around. It's generally tall and upright; something that will hold its shape throughout the year—a dwarf fruit tree, blueberry shrub, hot pepper plant, or chard, for example. Fillers are mid-height plants with a mounding habit. They often have great texture, color, or flowers—such as chives, sage, basil, or pansies and other edible flowers. Spillers are trailing or creeping plants that balance the planting by adding a nonlinear, unpredictable element. Dwarf peas, trailing nasturtiums, and strawberries are some of my favorite spillers.

Edible Landscapes

In an edible landscape, some, most, or all the plants produce food. The design can be as basic as tucking a few herbs, veggies, and edible flowers into an existing

Artichokes are large, sculptural plants that provide interest and structure in an edible landscape.

Red cabbage takes center stage in an informal, mixed ornamental and edible bed.

ornamental border, or as complex as creating a yard teeming with double-duty plants that are as bountiful as they are beautiful.

Gardeners who choose to create an edible landscape often do so because they prefer flowing curves, a casual or eclectic look, or a natural appearance to the straight lines and right angles of a traditional vegetable plot.

Edible landscaping can be a good option for growing food in front yards and other conspicuous locations. In the front yards of most neighborhoods, rows of cabbages would raise eyebrows, while artfully (and sparingly) placed cabbages—used as part of an ornamental edible border—would be considered charming. The difference is in the approach.

In designing an edible landscape, take cues from successful ornamental gardens. The best edible landscapes use the same principles, but in a different way. Think about a typical single-family home on an urban lot. Using edible landscaping principles, the trees would bear fruit or nuts, the shrubs would produce berries, and the flowers would be edible. Perhaps grapevines or kiwifruit would clamor up an arbor, with swaths of grains, herbs, sunflowers, and pumpkins edging the house.

Fruit and nut trees, berry shrubs, and perennial herbs and vegetables make the best candidates for edible landscaping, while attractive annual vegetables and edible flowers are wonderful supporting players.

Ornamental Edibles

Here is just a short list of the edibles attractive enough to be included in—or even the focus of—an ornamental container or garden bed.

amaranth	chives	lemongrass	rose
apple	cilantro	lettuce	rosemary
artichoke	dill	marjoram	runner beans
bachelor's buttons	eggplant	mint	sage
basil	fennel	nasturtium	shiso
beans	fig	orach	sorrel
beets	flax	oregano	squash
blueberry	fruit trees	parsley	strawberries
borage	grapes	passionflower	sunflower
cabbage	Jerusalem artichoke	peppers	sweet bay
chamomile	kale	plum	thyme
calendula	lavender	rhubarb	
chard	leeks		

Who says a vegetable garden has to be ▶ relegated to the back yard?

Planning for Planting

Think about your dream garden. What is growing there? Do you imagine stepping barefoot onto your deck to pluck sweet, juicy raspberries for your ice cream? Can you taste the crunch of fresh-picked sugar snap peas? Smell basil's spicy scent as you brush against it?

Everyone who imagines a garden has a few must-have plants in mind—those that say "summer!" or "dinner on the patio!" But the edibles you love may not love you back, and when you work within a small space, every plant must earn its place.

As you decide what to grow, my hard-earned advice is this: resist the temptation to head off to the nursery and browse. It is too easy to drop a day's pay on seeds or plant starts, and then get home and realize you bought enough to start a small farm. So before you start shopping, do some planning. If you're not the organized type, this can be the toughest part of growing a food garden. However, a certain level of planning is not only worth it, but mandatory. You will save money, get more out of your garden, and enjoy the process more if you take a few evenings to plan your garden before you plant.

◀ A winter's evening spent dreaming about the coming summer soon turns into more fun than work.

What Should I Grow?

Make a list of everything you want to grow. If you have big dreams, make that list a long one. For now, don't let pesky details hold you back—such as the fact that rooftops are not usually considered appropriate places to grow asparagus. If you want to grow it, put it on the list.

Plant what you love to eat. If you don't like squash, don't plant it simply because gardens are supposed to have squash or (one of my personal weaknesses) because it looks good on the seed package.

Consider how you spend money. For example, if you often pony up a few bucks a shot for those little plastic containers of herbs at the grocery store, herbs are probably a must-grow.

Unusual heirloom tomato cultivars are fun to grow because they aren't readily found in stores.

Note which edibles are hard to find in stores. Unusual edibles such as sprouting broccoli are easy to grow at home. Think about choosing plants that are not available through mass-market retailers, such as heirloom fruits and vegetables.

Consider that harvests aren't just for summer. Given the right conditions and a little effort, gardeners in most locales can enjoy harvests before and after the summer months—some year-round. Check your zone and look for crops with extended growing seasons.

Remember what tastes best fresh from the garden. All crops taste better fresh picked, but some, such as corn, really aren't worth eating any other way.

Know which conventionally grown produce has high residual pesticide levels. Consider crops from the "dirty dozen" list and slash your pesticide intake—and your grocery bill—by growing your own organics.

After you have created an impressive list, it's time for a reality check; it may be impossible to grow absolutely everything on your list during the same growing season. Don't cross anything off just yet though; you might decide to find another place to grow, or perhaps wait until next year to try the crops that you don't plant this year. Ask yourself a few more questions.

What will thrive in my space? A plant might look great in someone else's garden, but will it grow in yours? Think about your site assessment and consider how your site conditions might affect what you can grow. For example, if your balcony gets only three hours of sunlight daily, you should look for another place to grow tomatoes and other sun lovers.

Do I have time to look after it? Although a small garden will not demand hours of tending every day, there is no such thing as a no-maintenance garden. Some crops, such as berries, spinach, peas, and beans, require almost daily harvesting for peak flavor and so they continue to produce—or because, like radishes, they go from up-and-coming to has-been in three seconds flat. Plant low-maintenance crops such as potatoes or perennial vegetables if your busy life tends to keep you away from the garden.

What will be easy to grow? Avoid fussy crops when planting your first garden. Stick with beginner basics until your thumbs green up—you'll have a better chance at success, and will be more likely to stick with it.

Which edibles will produce the most amount of food in a limited space? Artichokes are gorgeous plants (and so tasty with a bit of melted butter). But they are also enormous and may produce only one choke per plant. Do you really want to devote half your space to half a meal? Think about making the best use of limited space. In the plant entries later in this book, look for edible varieties and cultivars that I've tagged as Suited to Small Spaces: particularly good choices for small gardens.

What's good for my soil? For a number of reasons, you should avoid planting the same crops in the same space year after year. Plants take the nutrients they need from the soil. If you plant the same thing in the same place repeatedly, those specific nutrients will eventually be exhausted. Just look at conventional agriculture's practice of monocropping (growing the

The Dirty Dozen Plus

For over a decade, researchers at the Environmental Working Group (ewg.org), a research and advocacy organization, have analyzed pesticide-testing data generated by scientists at the U.S. Department of Agriculture and federal Food and Drug Administration. Based on this data, EWG has developed an annually updated list of around twelve crops called the Dirty Dozen—conventionally produced fruits and vegetables that consistently test higher for levels of pesticide residues. The following edibles make up the most recent list.

apples	nectarines
blueberries	(imported)
celery	peaches
cherry tomatoes	spinach
cucumbers	strawberries
grapes (imported)	summer squash
hot peppers	sweet bell peppers
kale/collard greens	

Lettuce meets all my qualifications for a perfect crop. I use a lot of it, and it tastes best straight from the garden. It's also fast growing, attractive, space efficient, and easy to grow.

same crop on the same land year after year) to see the results: an ever-increasing reliance on chemical fertilizers. Crop rotation helps maintain healthy soil and plants.

Plant Families

A number of factors impact what you eventually plant and grow. One of the best ways to answer some of these questions is to have a basic knowledge of plant families.

Every plant has a Latin, or botanical, name. Three of those names—the species, genus, and family—are good to know when buying seeds or seedlings, because common names can vary from place to place.

Botanical naming can get quite complicated, but we're just going to focus on family names here. Once you know the plant's family, you can surmise many things about its

Runner beans and summer squash are both attractive and easy to grow.

soil and climate preferences, potential pests and diseases, the way it flowers and sets seed, and what you could plant beside it for best results.

Naturally, there are hundreds of plant families, but a few are especially important for food gardeners to know.

The alliums (Alliaceae)

Thank goodness for alliums. Not only do chives, garlic, leeks, onions, scallions (green onions), and shallots play a crucial role in cookery, but their aromatic qualities offer pest protection to other crops, making them excellent companion plants in the garden.

CLIMATE Alliums are cool-season crops that prefer the damp, cool weather of spring and fall.

SOIL Most alliums are not fussy—just give them relatively fertile soil with good drainage.

GOOD COMPANIONS Alliums actually repel many pests because of their aromatic properties, making them a friend to crops that are susceptible to slugs and other leaf-eating pests. They are, however, susceptible to mildew and fungal infections, often caused by poorly draining soil or humid conditions during hot weather. Following an infected planting of alliums with brassicas can reduce mildew in the soil.

The amaranths (Amaranthaceae)

The amaranths are nutritious, delicious, and some of the most beautiful edibles you will ever grow. The amaranth family is a cool-season group of leaf and root crops that includes protein-rich grains amaranth and quinoa, container-friendly cousins beet (or beetroot) and chard (also known as Swiss chard and silver beet), and versatile spinach.

Alliums, such as onions, make good companion plants to many other vegetables because of their pest-repelling qualities.

CLIMATE With the exception of amaranth itself, which thrives in warm weather, amaranths are at their peak during the cool weather of spring and fall. Some will bolt in the heat of summer, but many will happily weather winter's worst.

SOIL Good soil preparation is key to growing these crops. They prefer fertile, moist, well-drained soil that is rich in organic matter.

GOOD COMPANIONS Umbellifers such as fennel help to attract beneficial insects that prey on leaf miners and other pests that plague members of Amaranthaceae. Alliums and other aromatics repel slugs and other bandits.

Colorful Swiss chard is a member of the family Amaranthaceae.

The brassicas (Brassicaceae)

The family Brassicaceae is huge and diverse and includes arugula (rocket), Asian greens, broccoli, Brussels sprouts, cabbage, cauliflower, Chinese cabbage, collards, kale, kohlrabi, mizuna, mustard, radishes, rutabagas, and turnips—to name a few.

CLIMATE Another family in the cool-and-damp camp, some brassicas bolt in hot weather. Many will easily overwinter, becoming sweeter after cold weather and frost. Their insectary flowers (attractive to beneficial insects) are edible.

SOIL With so much diversity, a brassica is available for every soil type. They tend to prefer moist, well-drained, fertile, slightly alkaline soil with plenty of organic matter.

Radish is an easy-to-grow brassica that works well in terrace and rooftop gardens.

GOOD COMPANIONS Brassicas play nice with most other families, bringing pollinators to the garden with their flowers and helping alliums battle mildew. Interplant with aromatics to discourage pests.

The cucurbits (Cucurbitaceae)

The cucurbit family contains garden favorites cucumber, melon, pumpkin, squash, and zucchini. These warm-season annual bushes and vines have hairy stems and large, edible flowers. Many can be trained up trellises or along railings, making them great small-space producers.

CLIMATE These tropical natives love warm temperatures and lots of sun. (Can you blame them?)

SOIL Fertile, moist, well-drained soil is a must.

GOOD COMPANIONS The cucurbits' broad leaves provide great shade for heat-shy plants and shield the soil, preventing surface evaporation. Their spiny stems and leaves repel many pests and are traditionally used to keep raccoons and squirrels out of corn patches.

The legumes (Fabaceae)

The legume family includes peas, lentils, peanuts, snap beans, soybeans, and broad beans. In addition to the tasty seedpods and seeds produced by legumes, they are useful in the garden because they fix nitrogen in the soil via a symbiotic relationship with bacteria. The bacteria attaches to a plant's roots as small nodules, turning nitrogen pulled from the air into usable nitrogen for the plant and releasing it into the soil when the plant dies.

Squash, a cucurbit, grows in a community garden next to an unused railroad track

CLIMATE From cool-season (and even overwintering) choices such as peas and broad beans, to warm-season crops such as pole beans, this family thrives in a wide range of climates.

SOIL Legumes are fairly easygoing as long as the soil is well drained.

GOOD COMPANIONS Because of their relationship with nitrogen-fixing bacteria, legumes will improve nitrogen levels in your soil, making them an excellent choice to plant with, or prior to, crops that benefit from high nitrogen. Legumes play a crucial role in crop rotation and cover cropping for this reason.

The nightshades (Solanaceae)

If you automatically think "deadly" when you hear the word "nightshade," there is good reason. Solanaceae contain varying levels of a mild toxin known as belladonna. Even so, this family includes such kitchen staples as tomatoes, potatoes, eggplants, and hot and sweet peppers. Belladonna is mainly found in the flowers, leaves, and stalks, which humans have largely learned to avoid—except for one of the most deadly nightshade crops: tobacco.

CLIMATE With the exception of the humble potato, which can be grown just about anywhere, nightshades do best in hot, sunny conditions.

Whether snap, snow, or shelling, all peas are members of the legume family and are related to beans and peanuts.

Peppers, an easy nightshade to grow, can be planted in hanging containers to save space.

SOIL Nightshades are fairly easygoing when it comes to soil, although they dislike heavy soils with poor drainage.

GOOD COMPANIONS Any pollinator-attracting, pest-repelling plant is a friend to nightshades. Aromatic herbs such as basil and oregano are traditionally planted with tomatoes to improve the flavor of the fruit.

The umbellifers (Apiaceae)

The old botanical name for this family is Umbelliferae. Umbellifer has the same root as the word umbrella, which this family's flowers resemble. Carrots, celery, cilantro, dill, fennel, parsley, and parsnips are members. In addition to being good eating, they have tremendous value in the garden as insectary (beneficial insect-attracting) plants.

CLIMATE Like alliums and brassicas, umbellifers are a cool-season crop, with some members being among the most cold-hardy edibles. They prefer full sun.

SOIL Although most umbellifers do not require especially fertile soil, they grow best in soil that is loose and drains freely. Most are intolerant of acidic soil.

GOOD COMPANIONS Because of their aromatic and insectary properties, umbellifers are great companions to any crop that benefits from the pollinators they attract and the pests they repel. Nightshades are a classic companion.

With its wide range of culinary uses, attractive form, and tolerance for many growing conditions, parsley is one of the most commonly grown umbellifers.

Annuals, Biennials, and Perennials

One of the most basic distinctions for all plants is whether they are annual, biennial, or perennial.

As the name suggests, annual edibles are planted and harvested all within a year. Most common vegetable crops are annuals or are grown as annuals.

Unlike annuals, perennials return year after year without much—if any—help from you. Asparagus and rhubarb are the most commonly grown perennial vegetables in temperate climate gardens, but dozens of less well-known perennial vegetables are worthy of garden space. Fruit trees and shrubs are perennial, as are several herbs. They last for years—even decades—and once established tend to require little maintenance.

Biennials such as carrots, onions, cabbage, parsley, and beets complete their life cycle in their second year. Plant them and harvest their crops the same year, but collect their seeds the next. Knowing which plants are biennials is relevant only if you want to save the seeds they produce. Because saving and planting the seeds of biennial plants

Cool-Season vs. Warm-Season Vegetables

Cool-season vegetables enjoy the more moderate temperatures and damp weather that often accompany early spring, late summer, and autumn. Some will even survive frost, and in areas with mild winters they can be harvested all winter long. Cool-season edibles are typically grown for their leaves or roots, and include favorites such as beets, carrots, lettuce, peas, and scallions, among others.

Cool-season crops are the first to go in the ground come spring, and the last to be planted in summer or fall for a winter harvest. Many quick-maturing types can bookend your warm-season (main) crops to get the maximum use out of a particular bed, and most make good candidates for the winter garden.

In contrast, warm-season vegetables need heat and longer days to produce and ripen fruit. Being sensitive to cold, they must be planted well after spring's last frost. In climates with short growing seasons, cultivating warm-season vegetables can be challenging. Look for vegetables with a low number of days to maturity (noted on the seed packet) to ensure that your plants have time to ripen before the weather turns cool. Warm-season edibles include beans, cucumber, eggplant, melon, peppers, summer and winter squash, and tomatoes.

Patty pan squash is a warm-season vegetable.

Carrots and beets are both biennials. If you are collecting their seeds, you must wait until their second year.

can be a little complicated, most gardeners treat them as annuals, buying and planting new seeds each year.

Growing Fruit

Sweet or tangy, fruit makes a succulent addition to any garden. But while some fruits, such as strawberries, are easy to grow and require practically no care, tree fruits need a long-term commitment to pest control and pruning.

Whether you're drawn to kiwi, blueberries, or figs, researching appropriate varieties for your climate and site is crucial. Check the plant entries in this book, talk to an expert at your local nursery, or search online for

Trees and woody shrubs such as gooseberry are long-lived perennials.

Staking a Fruit Tree

Many young fruit trees should be staked as they are planted; ask the nursery if this is the case when you purchase a tree. Depending onto which rootstock they were grafted, some trees will require a permanent stake; others will need staking for a few years, or until they are well established.

The most common method of staking is to use two tall stakes—one on either side of the tree—with the tree supported in the middle. Drive the stakes into the ground in the undisturbed soil outside the planting hole. You can attach the tree to the stakes using wire or rope, and protect the tree from damage by wrapping the wire or rope in thick fabric or rubber (placing the wire or rope inside a piece of old garden hose works well). Place the supports as low as possible, and no more than two-thirds the height of the tree. Leave a little slack in the wire or rope so that the tree can move about in the wind slightly and thus develop a strong trunk and roots.

Old garden hose is put to good use protecting the bark of this staked tree.

49

recommended selections. Choosing a suitable variety is half the battle. Keep in mind that some fruits, including many varieties of apples and blueberries, require a compatible cultivar for adequate pollination. Choose a self-fruitful variety, or be prepared to plant two or more different types of the same fruit.

When growing fruit trees or shrubs, site selection and preparation are additional keys to success. While some berry plants can get by with part sun, fruit trees will struggle; always site them in your sunniest spot. All fruiting plants appreciate fertile, well-drained soil that is rich in organic matter. Cane fruits, such as raspberries and blackberries, require staking and trellising; ideally, you should install these supports prior to planting.

While strawberries often produce fruit the year they are planted and blackberries and raspberries produce the next year, fruit trees may not fruit until upwards of their fourth year.

Growing Herbs

If edible gardening is an addiction, herbs are a gateway drug. Most herbs are attractive and compact, making them ideal for containers and edible landscaping. They're easy to grow and maintain, therefore great beginner choices. They are also incredibly useful in cooking, cocktail making, and tea drinking, as well as in the garden— their aromatic qualities help repel pests. Another bonus: all culinary herbs have edible flowers. In short, they're good plants to have around.

Many of our most popular cooking herbs—marjoram, oregano, rosemary, sage, and thyme—are low-maintenance perennials with Mediterranean origins. Others—such as basil, cilantro, dill, parsley, and shiso—can be grown as annuals, replanted yearly from seed or start. Bay laurel, another culinary staple, is technically a small evergreen tree. With such a variety of options and uses available, herbs should be on everyone's must-grow list.

Herbs are a great choice for container gardening on a deck, patio, or balcony.

Where and When to Plant

After you understand the needs and preferences of the plants on your list, it's time to find a place for them in your garden.

Where?

I like to sketch out my garden—essentially a collection of various-sized containers—and assign plants to each pot. If you have an inground garden or use large containers for your garden, you can plant edibles with similar needs next to each other. Even in pots, many complementary plants perform better grouped together. When you are deciding where to plant, or to place your containers, keep the following in mind.

- **Height.** How tall will this plant grow? If you plant it in front of a shorter edible, it may grow to shade the smaller plant (which may or may not be a bad thing, depending on the shaded plant). Some edibles, such as amaranths and lettuces, like a little shade in hot weather.

- **Sun.** How much sun does the plant need? If your outdoor space offers varying levels of sunshine, place sun lovers where they can take advantage of the greatest amount of sunshine, and put shade-tolerant edibles in areas that receive less sun.

- **Support.** Will the plant require physical support, or can it be grown upward for the greatest use of space? Vine tomatoes usually need staking to keep them from keeling over. Kiwis and grapes require sturdy supports. Peas, pole beans, and some squash and melons can be grown up trellises or other structures to make the most of vertical space. Position these plants to take advantage of railings or walls that could act as supports.

- **Shelter.** Is the plant prone to rain-induced blights or diseases? If your growing area is sheltered by a roof overhang or other shelter, situate your tomatoes underneath to help them stay clear of blight. If your balcony or rooftop is prone to heavy winds, place plants with delicate foliage in the shelter of windbreaks.

When?

To organize your planting schedule for the year, take a look at your list of edibles and note when each one should be planted, indicating whether you will sow seeds or transplant seedlings (either bought from a nursery or raised from seed indoors). Seed-starting dates can be found on the seed packets. Plug these dates into your calendar so you never miss your window for planting.

I also like to create a simple chart outlining what I will plant and harvest across the seasons. If a year-round harvest is your aim, this can help you modify your planting list to fill any empty spots. You can download a blank chart for planning your garden at heavypetal.ca/freebies/.

This up-front work can seem a bit daunting. But with good planning, you will reap the bounty of a healthy, productive edible garden. And if you plan early in the season—before you feel rushed to get things in the ground—you'll appreciate the process even more.

The following chart provides general guidelines for planting and harvesting common herbs and vegetables.

Planting and Harvesting Times

Use this chart to get a sense of when to plant your annual herb and vegetable crops. Exact planting dates will vary by region and climate; adjust to suit your location and the weather at hand. Sow most seeds under cover until risk of frost has passed. Government organizations such as the U.S. National Climatic Data Center or Environment Canada track these dates and make them available online (search "average frost dates" or "growing season length" along with your zip code or region). ■ sow ■ harvest

When to Sow and Harvest Annual and Biennial Edibles

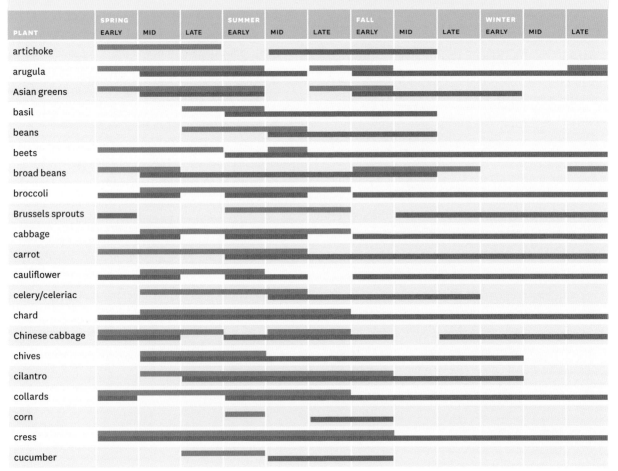

PLANT	SPRING EARLY	MID	LATE	SUMMER EARLY	MID	LATE	FALL EARLY	MID	LATE	WINTER EARLY	MID	LATE
artichoke												
arugula												
Asian greens												
basil												
beans												
beets												
broad beans												
broccoli												
Brussels sprouts												
cabbage												
carrot												
cauliflower												
celery/celeriac												
chard												
Chinese cabbage												
chives												
cilantro												
collards												
corn												
cress												
cucumber												

PLANT	Spring Early	Spring Mid	Spring Late	Summer Early	Summer Mid	Summer Late	Fall Early	Fall Mid	Fall Late	Winter Early	Winter Mid	Winter Late
dill			■	■	■	■	■	■	■			
eggplant			■	■	■	■	■	■				
endive	■	■	■	■	■	■	■	■	■			
fennel		■	■	■	■	■	■	■	■			
garlic	■			■	■		■	■	■			
kale	■	■			■	■	■	■	■	■	■	■
kohlrabi		■	■	■	■	■	■	■	■			
leeks	■	■	■	■		■	■	■	■	■	■	■
lettuce	■	■	■	■	■	■	■	■	■	■	■	■
melon				■		■	■	■				
okra				■	■	■	■					
onions (bulb and shallot)		■			■	■	■	■	■	■	■	■
onions (green and scallions)		■	■	■	■	■	■					
parsley			■			■	■	■	■	■	■	■
parsnip	■	■	■	■	■			■	■	■	■	■
peas	■	■	■	■			■	■				■
peppers and hot peppers			■	■		■	■	■				
potato	■	■	■		■	■	■					
radicchio	■	■	■	■	■	■						
radish	■	■	■	■		■	■	■	■			■
rutabaga				■	■	■	■	■				
spinach	■	■	■	■	■		■	■	■	■	■	■
summer squash and zucchini			■	■	■	■	■					
sweet potato			■	■		■	■	■				
tomato			■	■	■	■	■					
turnip		■	■	■	■	■	■	■				

Building Your Garden

After you have chosen a site and a garden style, it's time to think about how you want to build your garden. This chapter details the best methods of creating growing space, from choosing containers, to building raised beds, to no-till sheet mulching.

◄ Reward visitors to your vegetable garden with an engaging blend of containers and plant choices.

Containers vs. Inground Gardening

For many, growing in the ground is not an option. But if it is, you might wonder which is the better choice. Both have advantages and disadvantages.

While container gardens offer flexibility, portability, and fewer weeds, plants grown in containers are more dependent on you, the gardener, for their survival. Plants grown in the ground have greater access to water and nutrients via organic matter in the soil. In addition, gardeners can continually improve the health of their inground garden's soil by adding organic matter (such as compost, manure, or shredded leaves).

Not so with containers. For plants grown in pots, it's wise to use potting soil, a sterile growing medium that may or may not contain actual soil. Potting soil is designed to promote air and water circulation, but not necessarily plant growth. Because potting soil is often devoid of nutrients, container-grown plants require more frequent fertilizing, usually in the form of a biweekly liquid organic feeding.

Containers are a great option if your native soil has poor drainage, is polluted, or is otherwise lacking. You can have perfect soil in a container, and even customize it for a specific plant's preferences (sandy soil for carrots, for example, or acidic soil for blueberries).

Testing your soil

One important factor in deciding whether to plant in containers or directly in the ground (if you have the option) is

Repetition and symmetry work to make this patio container garden a modern, comfortable space.

what may have been on your land before you. Pollutants from previous residents or activities may still be present in the soil.

If you suspect contamination, you can have your soil tested by delivering or sending a sample to a soil lab. If there are potentially harmful substances present, container gardening allows you to control—and optimize—the soil in which your garden grows.

Choosing Containers

Almost anything that can hold soil can be home to a plant. Think beyond the garden center; an old metal wash bucket can go nicely with a cottage garden theme, or a lime green, straight-sided trash bin can punch up a '60s mod-style patio. If you are looking at pots specifically designed for planting, though, keep in mind various materials and the considerations that go with them.

Fiberglass. Fiberglass is a relative newcomer to the container game. Lightweight and fairly durable, fiberglass planters are usually designed to mimic stone, terra-cotta, or other types of containers—not always well. When done right, however, fiberglass can be a decent and affordable option. As with all planters, quality matters: cheap fiberglass can buckle, lose its shape, or actually melt.

Glazed ceramic. A huge range of color and style options are available in glazed ceramics. Designs range from simple to intricate, and colors tend to be deeply hued, lending richness to the garden. What's not to love?

Glazed ceramic pots come in every size and color, but watch their weight when filled with plants and soil.

Their weight, for one thing. Filled with soil, ceramic pots (and terra-cotta, for that matter) can be quite heavy. Depending on the temperature at which it was fired, a ceramic container may or may not survive a cold winter freeze; ask before you buy. Vietnamese-made ceramics can usually handle extremely cold weather.

Metal. From chic stainless steel to lightweight zinc, metal planters come in a wide variety of materials and styles. Although they usually look fabulous and last for years, metal containers absorb heat, causing soil to dry out quickly and potentially burning plants' roots. Because of this, metal planters are unsuitable as a container choice for sunny spots—unless they can be modified. Place a thick layer of insulating material, such as bubble wrap, sheets of cardboard, or something similar, between the container and soil to keep the soil from getting too hot and damaging sensitive roots. Alternatively, nest a slightly smaller plastic pot inside the metal container. Zinc containers, often the cheapest of the bunch, will rust over time and should be treated with rust paint if you want them to last. Because they are so lightweight they can buckle or tip easily.

Plastic and resin. Although plastic has become unfashionable these days, it does have its uses in the garden. Plastic is the cheapest, most lightweight container material, which is definitely a selling feature, especially for balcony gardens with weight restrictions. Resin and polyethylene are often used to make some decent-looking (if pricey) containers, which are said to resist fading resulting from sun exposure, unlike most plastics. Plastic, polyethylene, and resin all stand up to cold weather.

Grow bags. These flexible containers come in a variety of sizes, styles, and decorative colors. Some are designed to suit a specific type of crop, such as potatoes or tomatoes; others are designed to be wall-mounted for vertical growing. The durable fabric breathes, keeping soil aerated and warm but not too hot, and preventing overwatering. Fold flat for easy storage in the off-season.

Terra-cotta. Classic terra-cotta clay pots are popular for a reason: they are inexpensive, good-looking, and widely available. Terra-cotta wicks water away from the soil, which is great for Mediterranean herbs and other plants that tolerate dry conditions. It's not so great, however, for plants that like evenly moist soil, and a hot deck or sunny position can exacerbate this drying effect—you sign up for double water duty if you choose this route. One last thing about terra-cotta: because of its porosity, it absorbs water, which can cause it to crack in below-freezing temperatures. These pots should not remain outside year-round in areas with cold winters.

Wood. Infinitely customizable, wood can be styled to suit any garden. Although mass-produced wooden planter boxes all tend to have a similar look, wood can swing many ways. Use rough, reclaimed timbers for affordable, sustainable, rustic style, or use smooth-sanded and oiled slats for a container worthy of any craftsperson.

When building your own planter box, choose a naturally rot-resistant wood such as cedar. Applying tung or linseed oil will help protect wood from moisture. Or you can coat the wood with an eco-stain for longer lasting effects. Never use treated wood; it contains toxic chemicals that can leach into soil.

Terra-cotta pots lend a charming ambience, though keeping soil moist isn't their strong suit.

Preparing and Planting a Container

Planting a container isn't rocket science, but there are a few tricks of the trade that will help get you—and your plants—off to a great start.

MATERIALS

Container

Water

Premium organic potting soil or container mix

Coffee filter or small, fine screen (optional)

High speed electric drill with ½- to ⅝-in. drill bit (for containers without a drainage hole)

(additionally, for recycled containers)

Hydrogen peroxide or bleach

Stiff brush

1 If container is being repurposed, you will need to **clean and sterilize** it. Mold, disease, and fungi can lurk in used containers, which can then infect your healthy new plants. Sterilization is critical for pots in which you intend to start seeds, because seedlings are susceptible to a fungal disease known as damping-off, which can be transferred through contaminated pots.

To clean a pot, first remove any dirt or plant debris. Rinse the container, and then soak it overnight in a solution of water and hydrogen peroxide or bleach. (A 1:9 ratio of hydrogen peroxide or bleach to water ought to do the trick.) Scrub the pot with a stiff brush if necessary, rinsing thoroughly to remove any traces of cleaning agents, and then set it aside to dry.

If container is new, proceed directly to step 2.

2 **Provide drainage**. Good drainage is essential to healthy container crops. Unfortunately, the containers we fall in love with don't always come with drainage holes, but adding one is relatively simple.

Turn the container upside down. Using an electric drill, drill a single hole in the center of a small pot, or three or more holes in a large container. Press gently as you drill; too much force could crack the container. Choose a masonry or ceramic drill bit for terra-cotta or ceramic pots; plastic and metal containers can be tackled with a standard bit.

Many gardening books and magazines recommend adding a layer of so-called drainage material (shards of broken pots, sand, gravel) to the bottom of containers before planting. I favor skipping the added layer and focusing on providing soil that promotes good drainage. Placing a coffee filter or fine screen over the drainage hole can help prevent soil loss.

3 **Position your container**. Trust me: you do not want to lift the pot once it is full of soil. Place it as near to its final position as possible.

4 **Add soil to the container**. Look for a premium organic potting soil or container mix. Specially blended potting mixtures are lighter than standard garden soil and are designed to promote good air circulation and drainage.

5 **Plant**. Plant your seeds or seedlings according to the accompanying instructions.

6 **Water and mulch**. Water in your newly planted seeds or plants. This will help settle the soil, which can sometimes take weeks to fully compress. Keep extra potting soil on hand to top off your containers. I like to top off my containers with an inch or two (2.5 to 5 cm) of rich, black, top-quality bagged soil or finished (completely broken down) compost. Not only does this provide nutrients and conserve moisture, but it also looks great.

To support healthy herbs and vegetables, pots needs drainage holes and good quality potting soil.

Gardening in Raised Beds

A raised bed, which is simply an elevated gardening bed, can be built using wood, stone, or concrete frames. Technically, an outer frame isn't necessary in a raised bed, but frames do help define the space and prevent soil from washing away.

Why go to the trouble of building a raised bed if you can simply garden in the ground? Raised beds have a number of advantages over traditional inground gardening.

If your native soil is polluted, compacted, or otherwise problematic, you can build a raised bed and bring in fertile soil customized for your specific needs. You can even build a raised bed in areas with no soil, such as on top of driveways and patios. (It is best to stick with regular containers for rooftops, decks, and other areas where direct soil contact might cause drainage or rot issues.)

In addition, the soil in raised beds warms up quicker in the spring, allowing you to get an early jump on the planting season. Since you don't walk in raised beds, you don't

Raised beds for vegetables now give the owners easy access to fresh, homegrown produce.

This little-used patch of lawn was prime for repurposing.

compact the soil (which can reduce its ability to absorb water). Raised beds also mean good drainage, assuming you use the appropriate soil—good news for those with boggy native conditions.

Finally, because they are elevated, raised beds are great for gardeners with mobility and back issues. They can even be designed so that you can access them while seated.

How to Build a Raised Bed

This bed is 3 by 6 ft. and 1 ft. deep, but the dimensions can be easily adjusted. Most raised beds are a maximum of 4 ft. wide to allow gardeners to reach into the center. Minimum depth for leafy veggies and herbs is 6 in.; for root vegetables, at least 12 in. Options include oiling or eco-staining the wood to extend its life, lining the bottom of the bed with mesh hardware cloth to keep out burrowing animals, fitting copper strips inside the bed's top edge to deter slugs, and installing PVC hoops to support row covers.

MATERIALS

Four 6-ft.-long, 2-by-6 untreated cedar wood boards

Four 3-ft.-long, 2-by-6 untreated cedar wood boards

One 4-ft.-long, 4-by-4 untreated cedar wood board, cut into four 11-in. lengths

Thirty-two 3½-in. #14 wood screws (deck screws are ideal)

(optional)

Linseed oil, tung oil, or eco-stain

Hardware cloth, 3 by 6 ft., cut to fit the bottom of the bed

One 18-ft. length of copper stripping

One 10-ft. length of 1-in. diameter PVC pipe, cut to four 11-in. lengths

Two 9-ft. lengths of ½-in. diameter PVC pipes

Eight 1-in. galvanized semicircular brackets, or metal strapping to fit

Sixteen ½-in. #8 wood screws

1 If you plan to oil or stain the boards, do this first, and allow a day or two for them to dry.

2 On a concrete patio or another level surface, set out two 11-in.-long, 4-by-4 boards and lay one of the 3-ft.-long, 2-by-6 boards on top, with the two 4-by-4 posts flush at each end.

3 Attach the board with a couple of 3½-in. screws.

4 Repeat with the second short board. Make two like this; these will be the short ends of the bed.

5 Stand these sides on edge and position the 6-ft.-long, 2-by-6 boards.

6 Attach these longer boards with screws.

7 Move your raised bed into place, leveling the surface if necessary.

8 (Optional) Attach copper strips along the inside top edge of the bed to deter slugs from crawling in, line the bottom with hardware cloth, and/or attach the PVC piping that will support row covers or shade cloth.

9 (Optional) To make row cover supports, attach two 11-in.-long pieces of the 1-in. diameter PVC pipe to the inside of each long side of the bed. Space the pipes 1 to 2 ft. from each end, and secure them with ½-in. screws and

semicircular brackets. These tubes will serve as the holders for the ends of the hoops you will insert if row covers are needed. To make hoops, bend the thinner, ½-in. diameter PVC pipes into semicircles, inserting the ends

into the larger, permanent pipes (you could also use flexible young branches).

10 Fill the bed with high-quality organic soil. For a less expensive option, use the sheet mulching method.

Attach two 3-ft.-long, 2-by-6 boards to the 4-by-4 corner posts.

Assemble the frame by attaching the longer 2-by-6s to the short ends.

You can attach the PVC pipes to support row covers, two for each long side, with metal strapping or brackets.

Finished beds are ready to be filled with soil.

Gardening in the Ground

For those with access to a small patch of earth, inground gardening is a quick and inexpensive way to get started. To prepare the space, there are two primary options: dig, or don't. Tilling is the traditional means of cultivation, and involves digging into the ground, removing vegetation, and making the soil ready for production. With sheet mulching, you build up rather than digging down, layering various types of organic materials over the area you want to plant. The layers break down to create a fertile garden plot.

Tilling

Although some gardeners almost never till or dig—because turning the soil can kill helpful microorganisms and damage soil structure—digging loosens and aerates soil, and lets you add organic matter and nutrients to soils that are compacted or otherwise lacking. If you choose to go this way, loosen the soil to a depth of about 6 to 10 in., incorporating compost or manure as you go.

Removing sod (grass or lawn) is a bit of an ordeal. I am not advocating for lawns, but do think about sheet mulching on top of grass instead of digging in, unless you're a big fan of blisters.

If you do need to get rid of sod, however, use a long-handled spade with a flat, sharp edge to cut the turf into sections. Then, using the spade like a pie server, jam it under a section of sod, slicing off the roots with the spade's sharp edge. Lift the sod away.

Sheet mulching involves layering organic materials, including carbon-rich matter such as straw.

Sheet Mulching in a Small Space

Even in just a few square feet, sheet mulching allows you to make your own rich soil using stuff that would otherwise be considered trash. The major drawback is the time it takes for the layers to break down—sometimes more than a year. However, you can get around this by topping decomposing layers with several inches of quality soil and planting shallow-rooted crops.

MATERIALS

Frame materials (optional)

Flat cardboard (uncolored, with all tape and staples removed) or 10+ sheets of newspaper (black and white)

Straw, dry leaves, wood chips (carbon-rich organic material)

Grass clippings, non-animal kitchen scraps, coffee grounds, manure (nitrogen-rich organic material)

Compost or topsoil

1 **Prepare the site**. If the soil is not compacted, begin by cutting back any existing lawn or vegetation and marking the outline of your future garden. If the soil is compacted, begin by loosening it.

2 **Construct a frame** (optional) to define your garden. A frame isn't necessary, but it will help prevent soil loss through erosion. Place the frame in its final position.

3 **Lay down cardboard or newspaper**. This is the first layer, upon which you will build your soil. This layer will smother the grass or weeds below, so make sure you overlap the edges by at least 6 in. to prevent weeds from sneaking through. Water down this layer.

4 **Add a layer of carbon-rich organic matter**. Good sources of carbon tend to be brown, dry, or dead, such as straw, dry leaves, or wood chips. This layer should be about 6 in. deep.

5 **Add a layer of nitrogen-rich organic matter**. Nitrogen sources, such as unfinished compost, non-animal kitchen scraps, grass clippings, coffee grounds, and manure tend to be green or wet. Add a thin layer, 2 to 3 in. deep.

6 **Repeat steps 4 and 5**. Alternate layers of carbon-rich materials with layers of nitrogen-rich organic matter until your bed is about twice the desired height, ending with a layer of carbon-rich material.

7 **Water**. Soak the entire bed to start the decomposition process. Keeping the bed moist over the coming months will also help the layers break down quickly. After watering and a few weeks of decomposition, the bed will have shrunk in height considerably.

8 **Add soil**. Top the bed with a thick layer of compost or topsoil, about 4 in. deep.

9 **Plant**. Ideally, you will build your sheet-mulched bed a year before you intend to plant, giving the materials ample time to break down. If you need to plant immediately, however, your best bet is to choose shallow-rooted plants such as lettuce greens and cruciferous vegetables (broccoli, cauliflower).

Optimizing Your Soil

Many small-space gardeners know the importance of fertile soil, but don't feel a burning desire to learn the details of pH ratios and N-P-K balance. If you are one of these types, a simple understanding of the key role of organic matter, along with a commitment to keeping your soil rich in it, is plenty to get you a lovely harvest.

If, however, you truly want to make the most of your limited space by understanding the factors that will maximize its harvest, this is your chapter.

I grew up gardening alongside my parents and grandparents—experienced growers all. Gardening on my own, I went through the motions of making compost and mulching because I was supposed to. It wasn't until I took the time to learn about soil that I grasped why I was doing it.

Soil doesn't simply hold plants—it supports them. Thus, it is our job to support the soil and the myriad life forms that exist within it (which, in turn, help feed our plants).

◄ Healthy soil produces healthy plants. Building healthy soil is job one for organic gardeners.

What is Soil?

Soil is made up of minerals (eroded rock) and organic matter (decaying and well-decayed plant and animal matter).

Healthy soil is dark, rich, and crumbly. It smells sweet and, well, earthy. It is teeming with life: fungi, bacteria, and other microorganisms, and sometimes insects and earthworms. Although mineral content is important, it's the living part of the soil that fuels plant growth.

Soil pH

Soil pH indicates the acidity or alkalinity of your soil on a scale of 1 to 14, with 7.0 being neutral. Soil with a pH lower than 7.0 is acidic, greater than 7.0 is alkaline. Most edible plants prefer soil that is neutral to slightly acidic. In very acidic or very alkaline soil, plants have difficulty accessing nutrients. You can test the pH of your soil using a kit obtained from a garden center or by sending a soil sample to a lab.

While there are specific amendments that can address pH-imbalanced soils (lime or wood ash if it's too acidic, sulfur for overly alkaline), perhaps the easiest remedy is adding organic matter. The buffering ability of supplements like compost, leaf mulch, and manure helps to regulate pH, holding onto excess minerals and nutrients so they don't tip the balance.

Healthy soils are dark, rich, and full of organic matter.

Potatoes prefer an acidic soil with a pH below 6.0. Most vegetables will do well in soil with a pH of 6.0 to 7.2.

Soil texture

Texture refers to the mineral content of the soil—specifically, the size of the mineral particles in the soil and their relative proportion to one another.

Particles are classified by size, from smallest to largest, as clay, silt, and sand. The larger the particle size, the larger the air pockets (known as pores) between them. Pores allow water and air to move through the soil, which is why sandy soils drain quickly and clay soils tend to become hard and waterlogged. Silt falls somewhere between the two.

The goal for most gardens is soil with roughly equal proportions of sand, silt, and clay—along with a healthy dose of organic matter. This results in a magical substance called loam, which is what you want in your garden.

Loam is richer in nutrients than sand and drains better than silt and clay. It retains water, yet doesn't become waterlogged. In short, loam is the perfect soil for growing food. It takes time and work, but by regularly adding organic matter to your soil, you can create loam from even the sandiest or most clay-packed dirt.

Example of sandy soil, loam, and clay soil (from left to right).

The Organic Advantage

Organic growers know that healthy soil grows healthy plants that are stronger, more productive, and better able to fight off diseases and pests. These gardeners think in terms of growing the soil rather than the plants. In contrast, the nonorganic approach uses chemical fertilizers that provide a short-term boost to plants but do nothing to improve the soil. In fact, chemical fertilizers and pesticides actually harm the soil by disrupting the natural balance of soil-dwelling organisms.

Organic matter is the part of the soil that's alive—not just with microbes, bacteria, and other helpful organisms, but also with well-decayed and decaying plant and animal matter, which provides the fuel for these nutrient recyclers. It neutralizes the effects of wonky pH, improves soil structure and airflow, increases a soil's water-holding capacity while improving drainage, and provides the main source of nutrients for plants.

Is there anything organic matter cannot do? Not much. If you were to add nothing else to your garden but organic superstars such as compost, manure, worm castings, or leaf mulch, your garden would be happy. Luckily, organic matter is easy to come by, and, best of all, it's often free.

Soil for Containers Is Different

Most container garden soils are notably lighter than soils of inground gardens. If you put garden soil in pots (even if it started out rich and healthy) it would soon become hard and compact, suffocating your plants' roots.

The name potting soil is kind of misleading; standard potting soil contains very little—if any—actual soil. It comprises a variety of organic and inorganic materials that contribute essential qualities to the mix, such as good moisture and nutrient retention, and adequate drainage.

Traditional soilless potting mixes are usually made up of large quantities of peat moss combined with perlite (white, lightweight, puffed volcanic rock added to improve drainage), vermiculite (a heated mineral product that looks like fish scales, added to improve water-holding capacity), and/or sand (which also improves drainage).

Because they contain no soil, these potting mixes lack the living organisms that carry out the nutrient cycling that makes living soil function. And because microorganisms aren't doing the work of feeding the soil, you have to do it yourself. Mix in a handful or two of your own homemade compost or a granular organic fertilizer when planting. A biweekly liquid feed with a balanced organic fertilizer will also help keep things growing.

Container soil options

It is possible to purchase organic, soil-based potting soils; they usually contain compost, along with soil conditioners such as coir or perlite. Some excellent soil-based products are on the market—ask for a recommendation at a trusted garden center. Because these types of potting soils contain nutrient-rich compost, you won't have to fertilize quite so often.

Many gardeners custom blend their own potting soils using a mix of coir or peat, perlite, compost, and other soil amendments. Storing all those products can be a

Peat

Peat, or sphagnum, moss is a common ingredient in potting soil mixes. It acts like a sponge, holding water but draining freely. It's lightweight and holds nutrients well. It has a slightly acidic pH. Despite these positives, I do not recommend using potting soil that contains peat, because it is mined from ecologically sensitive bogs and wetlands. Look for a peat alternative such as coir. Coir is made from coconut hulls and is a sustainable peat substitute. Although it has little nutrient value, like peat it holds moisture well, lightens the soil, and promotes good air circulation.

challenge in small spaces, though. There is no shame in simply ripping open a bag of good quality potting soil.

Make sure you look for something labeled organic "container mix" or "potting soil"—do not buy topsoil. If in doubt, ask someone at a garden center you trust for a recommendation.

Compost

Using compost is arguably the single best thing you can do for your garden—not to mention that composting keeps a huge amount of waste out of landfills. Use compost as a mulch (spread it on top of the soil to keep weeds down, reduce evaporation and erosion, and build up soil nutrients), combine it with potting soil to create a killer container mix, or add a handful to planting holes before transplanting shrubs or starts.

Containers need specially blended soil that is designed to promote good air circulation and drainage.

Full of worms and microorganisms, compost is the ideal amendment for any soil.

Where to make compost if space is limited

Even if your outdoor space is tiny or high above the ground, it's possible to make usable compost. All you need is a small bit of yard, a bin designed especially for composting, a planter on your deck, or even just a box under your sink. Successful compost requires air, moisture, and a good balance of organic waste materials.

In an open pile. If you have a small corner of yard, building an unenclosed compost pile is the easiest way to make compost (and I'm all for minimal effort). Just pile up your greens and browns and let them sit. Turn the pile occasionally. The downside to an open pile is that it can look messy and attract pests such as rodents, raccoons, or the dog next door.

In a bin. Dozens of ready-made compost bins are available and range from simple wooden constructions to circular plastic units designed for easy turning. They are almost always built with holes or slats to facilitate air circulation, and with flaps or doors near the bottom for removing the finished compost. Bins keep things tidy, help insulate your compost (which speeds up its decomposition), and protect its tasty morsels from foraging critters.

Many bins have open bottoms, which can make them challenging for patios or balconies. Look for a style with an enclosed bottom and set it on slats or blocks over a tray (there will be holes in the bottom for aeration, so some liquid will escape). You can make your own bin using a plastic garbage can,

What (and What Not) to Compost

Compostables are classified as green or brown. Green matter is wet and rich in nitrogen. Browns are dry and rich in carbon.

Brown Matter	Green Matter	Do Not Compost
Dry plant matter: dead plants, leaves, stalks, twigs, and grass	Coffee grounds and tea bags	Cooked food
Paper towels	Fresh grass clippings, leaves, and plant matter	Dog or cat feces
Pine needles	Hair (your pet's or yours, if it hasn't been chemically treated)	Diseased plants
Sawdust	Manure, aged (not cat or dog)	Fat or oil
Shredded newspaper or cardboard	Seaweed	Meat or fish
Straw or hay	Uncooked fruit and vegetable scraps	Perennial weeds or weeds that have gone to seed
Wood ashes	Washed eggshells	
Wood chips	Weeds that have not gone to seed	
Wine corks		

drilling holes around the sides and bottom. If you use a round container, you can aerate the contents by tipping it on its side (lid on) and rolling it back and forth.

As you go. Cut out the middleman by disposing of your kitchen and garden scraps in the spot you want to enrich. Using this composting-in-place method, you can create good soil by burying kitchen scraps (chopping up larger pieces) in a hole or trench in the garden or at the bottom of a large container. Bury the scraps with the soil you just removed. If you're adding scraps to a container, add a thick layer (6 in.) of garden or potting soil on top to prevent the scraps from smelling and attracting pests.

In a worm bin. Vermicomposting uses worms to turn your kitchen waste into quality compost. For gardeners without space for conventional composting, vermicomposting is the way to go. It takes little room; worms will live happily in a bin under your kitchen

How to Make Compost

Successful, nonstinky compost is made using a mixture of green stuff (wet, nitrogen-rich matter such as grass clippings and kitchen scraps) and brown stuff (dry, carbon-rich matter such as dead leaves and straw). Aim for a ratio of at least twice as much brown matter to green matter.

MATERIALS
Brown matter (see lists)
Green matter (see lists)
"Starter" compost, with worms and other decomposers (optional)

1 Start with a layer of brown matter. I like to use a thick layer (about 6 in.) of chopped up dead twigs or wood chips for the foundation; this allows for good air circulation at the bottom of the pile or bin.

2 Follow this with a layer of green matter: grass clippings, kitchen scraps and such. If you have a neighbor or gardening friend with good aged compost (preferably with worms and other decomposers), ask if you can use a bucketful to jumpstart your pile.

3 Alternate layers of greens and browns, not necessarily all at once, until your bin is full or you run out of materials. Try to finish with a layer of browns—exposed greens tend to attract pests.

4 Turn your compost (mix it up) at least several times a year, adding water if necessary (compost should be slightly damp, like a wrung-out sponge).

Air circulation speeds up the process of decomposition and prevents the compost pile from becoming stagnant. Depending on the size of your pile (larger piles heat up faster and thus finish more quickly), you can expect finished compost—rich, crumbly black humus—within a couple of months to a year.

sink. If you don't have room indoors for a bin 1 to 3 ft. wide and long, rethink the worm bin; worms should be protected from freezing temperatures, as well as temperatures above 86°F.

You can buy worm composters online, in garden centers, or even through forward-thinking city governments. You can also make your own by drilling holes in the lid, bottom, and sides of a plastic or wooden bin.

Worm bins need three ingredients: bedding for the worms (dampened, shredded newspaper works well), a scoop of garden soil to add grit and beneficial microorganisms, and worms, of course! Don't use earthworms from your garden; track down red wigglers or brandling worms (*Eisenia foetida*)—superstar

Cut up twigs and small-diameter branches so that they will break down faster.

Dry leaves are an excellent source of carbon, and they keep your compost from becoming too wet—and smelly.

You can buy special bins for holding kitchen waste until you have time to visit the compost pile—this one has a carbon filter in the lid to block odors. Ice cream buckets and large yogurt containers can also be used.

composters that can be found at bait shops and garden centers. They like tight spaces and eat their way through a lot more waste than do common garden worms.

Mulch

Next to adding compost, mulching is the best thing you can do for your soil. Mulch is a layer of material spread over the surface of your soil. Traditional mulches include straw, compost, leaf mold (leaf compost), and bark mulch, but plastic sheeting, cardboard and newspaper, pebbles, and even fabric can also be used.

Compost bins are not all that attractive, so look for an out-of-the-way spot, build a screen, or plant bright flowers—such as nasturtiums—to distract the eye.

Compost is the best mulch around. It not only suppresses weeds and limits evaporation, but it feeds the soil as its nutrients are carried in by worms and microbes.

Mulching keeps weeds at bay, protects the soil from erosion, reduces evaporation, and acts as an insulator to protect plants' roots in winter and to moderate the effects of hot summer temperatures. Using attractive mulches can give your containers or beds a freshly planted look.

If you use compost as mulch, it will do double duty—not only providing all the protective benefits, but adding nutritional advantages to the soil as well.

Aim to mulch your containers or garden beds at least twice a year: in spring to provide benefits during the active

Straw mulch suppresses weeds, prevents soil erosion and water evaporation, and keeps developing fruit out of direct contact with the soil.

Because it helps warm the soil, black plastic mulch is commonly used with plants that produce better in warmer temperatures. It is also an effective weed barrier.

growing season, and in fall to protect the soil over the winter. Spread a layer between 2 and 4 in. thick over the exposed surfaces of your soil. The mulch should not touch the stem or trunk of a plant; leave a little breathing room. Mulch that sits against stems and stalks traps moisture and can encourage disease and rot.

Fertilizers

I used to think that being an organic gardener only meant avoiding pesticides and chemical fertilizers. My plants were getting air, water, and sunlight—everything they got in the wild, right? Going natural meant I needn't add anything.

Wrong! Our small-space gardens are not natural eco-systems, replicating the growth, decomposition, and regrowth of a space in the wild. This means we must step in and provide some nutrients to our soil. The best way? You guessed it: adding compost. It's redundant but true— if you add nothing else to your garden but your own home-made compost, your soil will be happy.

So why are there a ton of fertilizers (organic and otherwise) sold at garden centers? Fertilizers are necessary in a couple of instances: when you run out of compost (there never seems to be enough) and when you are gardening in containers. Although containers benefit from a light mulching of compost, they also need supplemental feeding. Soil nutrients are constantly being taken up by the plants, which have less soil to draw from than if they were planted in the ground. And containers require more frequent watering, which leads to leaching and nutrient loss.

N-P-K

Three main nutrients are vital and form the basis for most fertilizers: nitrogen, phosphorus, and potassium, or N-P-K. Fertilizers display the ratio of these three elements on the package. For example, a complete (all-purpose) organic fertilizer might read 4-4-4, which tells us that it contains 4 percent nitrogen, 4 percent phosphorus, and 4 percent potassium.

If you know your soil has relatively balanced proportions of N, P, and K (for example, if you start with store-bought potting soil), a balanced, all-purpose fertilizer is a good bet. But if your soil lacks one or two of the major elements, or you want to apply a fertilizer for a specific purpose—say, to increase leafy green growth—you should know a little about what these elements do for your plants.

N (nitrogen). Nitrogen promotes foliage growth. Nitrogen-rich fertilizers are a good choice for getting seedlings off to a good start, and for leafy vegetables

Leafy greens such as Asian mesclun mix benefit from light feedings with a nitrogen-rich fertilizer.

throughout the season—but too much will create lush growth without fruit production. Natural sources include blood meal, alfalfa meal, cottonseed meal, and liquid fish emulsion.

P (phosphorus). Phosphorous is required for root development, disease resistance, and fruit and flower production. Applying a phosphorus-rich fertilizer just before a plant's fruiting stage optimizes fruit development. Natural sources include bone meal, rock phosphate, and seabird and bat guano (poop).

K (potassium). Potassium, or potash, is essential for overall plant health and is required throughout the growing season. Too little potassium results in poor yields and brown, curling leaves. Root crops respond

Because container soil usually includes minimal nutrients, container-grown plants need fertilizing throughout the growing season.

well to potassium. Natural sources include green-sand, kelp meal, and wood ash.

Applying supplements

Organic matter such as compost can be applied at any time, though spring is considered ideal. Dig it into the soil before planting your seeds or transplants, add a handful to planting holes, or use it as a mulch during the growing season whenever your plants need a boost.

Granular (powdered) fertilizers. Organic amendments such as blood meal, rock phosphate, greensand, or all-purpose mixes can be dug in a few weeks prior to or during planting. Applying fertilizer near the roots is optimal. You can also side dress (scratch a little into the soil around the base of a plant) during the growing season. The effects should last for a relatively long time, particularly with inground gardens.

Liquid fertilizers. These deliver nutrients efficiently and quickly and are ideal for container gardens. Liquid fish emulsion and liquid kelp are common, but you can also find fertilizers made from worm castings and other types of guano, and blood, feather, and bone meals. Most liquid fertilizers are mixed with water and applied once every one to two weeks during the growing season.

For all fertilizers, follow the instructions on the package carefully. Organic fertilizers are less likely to burn plants' roots because of the slow-release nature of organics; however, improper use of any fertilizer can harm plants.

Sowing and Growing

Starting seeds is easy, right? You just push a seed into the dirt. Sure, the *how* is simple, but the *when* requires a bit more thought.

Plant a seed too early, and cold temperatures will prevent it from germinating. Plant it too late, and it won't have time to grow up and produce fruit before winter chills hit. Catching that planting window is the key to seed-starting success.

◄ Everything is ready for bean seedlings to be transplanted in this terrace garden.

Of course, you don't have to grow all your edibles from seed: buying ready-to-plant starts from the nursery has its merits. Whichever route you choose, this chapter will teach you how to launch your garden. Use the planting chart included in this book to know which edibles to plant when.

From Seed or From Starts?

I never fail to be amazed by seeds—or the incredible bounty that I can harvest from what began as tiny, shriveled specks. Some beginning gardeners regard seed starting warily, but the fact is, seeds are designed to survive, thrive, and eventually reproduce. We simply help them along by providing a little loving care.

If you'd rather not start your own seeds, you can buy vegetable seedlings, also known as starts or transplants, from a nursery. But many gardeners start their plants from seeds for a couple good reasons. Seeds are almost always cheap, and sometimes free. You can get 500 lettuce seeds for the same price as a six-pack of lettuce transplants. Also, finding seeds for rarer vegetables is easier than finding transplants (think purple carrots and wrinkled heirloom tomatoes).

Plants started easily from seed (direct sowing)
- arugula
- Asian greens
- beans
- beets
- carrot
- chard
- Chinese cabbage
- cilantro
- collards
- corn
- dill
- fennel
- garlic
- kale
- kohlrabi
- lettuce
- mizuna
- mustard greens
- scallions
- parsnip
- peas
- potato
- radish
- rutabaga
- spinach
- turnip

Plants better started from seedlings (transplanting)
- artichoke
- asparagus
- blackberries
- blueberries
- Brussels sprouts
- celery
- currants
- eggplant
- fruit trees
- grape
- kiwi
- marjoram
- melon
- mint
- okra
- oregano
- peppers
- raspberry
- rhubarb
- rosemary
- sage
- sweet potato
- thyme
- tomato

Plants that can be started either way
- broccoli
- cabbage
- cauliflower
- chives
- cucumber
- leeks
- parsley
- squash
- strawberry

Plant-sowing preferences

Some plants are notoriously difficult to start from seed, or need to be started indoors in late winter. Unless you've got a decent grow light set up and a penchant for staying on top of watering chores, it's usually easiest to purchase these plants as seedlings. Others are easy to start from seed, or actually prefer being sown in ground because they dislike having their roots disturbed by transplanting.

Where to sow

You can sow seeds two ways: indoors in little pots (to be transplanted outdoors later), or outdoors in the place you want them to grow.

Starting seeds indoors can be more involved. But in many climates, crops such as tomatoes, melons, eggplants, and peppers need to be started indoors, because they require consistent warmth and a long growing season.

Not all seeds can or should be started indoors, however. Root crops such as carrots and beets do not like to be disturbed once they have, well, put down roots.

Seed packets often contain more seeds than you can use in a small garden, so coordinate your purchases with fellow gardeners and share them among friends.

Where to Get Seeds

Seeds are available from many sources, including the rack at the garden center. I do most of my seed shopping online. It allows me to think more clearly and not be tempted into grabbing random pretty seed packets. Online suppliers also often sell heirloom and specialty seeds not found elsewhere.

Seed-swapping events are great opportunities to share surpluses with other gardeners. Many botanical and community gardens facilitate these events. Seed swapping also happens online (search "swap seeds").

If you are purchasing at retail, look for seeds from a reputable local company. They likely produce seeds that are suited to your growing area. Also look at the sell-by date on the packet; make sure the seeds are intended for the current year. Choose organic seeds if possible; they will be adapted to organic growing conditions. Finally, if you want to save the seeds your plants produce at the end of the season, look for seeds marked "OP" (open-pollinated).

Seed needs

Seeds require moisture, warmth, light, and oxygen to germinate. But like most things in gardening, it all starts with the soil.

Soil. Seeds prefer a light, airy medium that provides good air circulation and allows for effortless root development; it should hold moisture but not get soggy.

If you are planting directly outdoors, give your planting bed a once-over with a cultivator to provide the loose, fine soil seeds require. This is also a good opportunity to amend your soil with compost or other organic supplement.

If you're starting seeds indoors, use a seed-starting mix: a light and fluffy, sterile blend of peat or coir, perlite, and vermiculite. A sterile mix is ideal, because garden soil and compost contain living organisms that can introduce diseases. They might also contain weed seeds.

Containers. You can start seeds in anything from recycled yogurt containers to store-bought plastic cell packs. Forget those cute little terra-cotta pots—they allow the soil to dry out too quickly, and ditto for compressed peat pellets.

Newspaper pots are great for plants that don't like to have their roots disturbed, since you can plant the entire pot. Find instructions online to make them yourself (search "newspaper seedling pots"), and

Larger seeds, such as beans, are easy to handle and plant.

Starting seeds indoors gives you a jump on the planting season.

make a free supply of seed-starting pots in no time. Plantable pots made of newspaper, coir, or other biodegradable material must be thin enough (and must break down fast enough) for plants' roots to be able to penetrate the walls with little effort.

Choose containers that will allow your seedlings room to develop, or be prepared to move plants into larger homes if they outgrow their pots before they are ready to go outside.

Moisture. Maintaining consistent moisture is crucial to success in seed starting. Your aim is to keep the soil consistently sponge-damp; fluctuating from bone-dry to sopping wet is torture to sensitive seedlings. Use a watering can with a fine rose nozzle, a spray bottle, or, even better, water from below. Place your pots in a tray or sink filled with 1 in. of water and let them soak it up. Don't let them sit in the water for too long—half an hour should do the trick.

Warmth. Some seeds, such as peas and other early-season vegetables, prefer cool soil. Others, such as peppers and cucumbers, prefer a slightly balmier climate. Most seeds germinate best in temperatures from 60° to 75°F.

Light. After seedlings have emerged from the soil, they need a lot of light; without it, they grow leggy—tall, thin, and weak. Providing the light they want—14 to 16 hours a day—will probably be your biggest challenge in indoor growing.

Planting seeds is a great project for kids.

Newspaper pots make great seed-starting containers, because you can plant the pot with the plant.

Fluorescent lighting is a great substitute for sunlight when starting seeds indoors.

You'd go mad trying to sow individual tiny seeds, such as those of carrots and lettuce. Just sprinkle a pinch onto the surface and scratch them into the soil.

A bright, sunny window will do, but this is not ideal (clouds plus early spring's lack of daylight hours equals a light deficiency). If you want to get serious about seed starting, you can set up your own operation using fluorescent lights. Believe it or not, a couple of 40-watt fluorescent tube lights will keep your seedlings happy and healthy.

Hang the light(s) from your ceiling, balance it on the backs of two chairs, mount it under a shelf—however you do it, make sure you can either move the light or the plants up and down. Start out with the light about 3 to 4 in. above the seed trays and gradually increase the distance to about 4 to 6 in. as your plants grow.

Feeding and Thinning Seedlings

A plant's cotyledon, or seed, leaves are first to emerge from the soil. These leaves provide the growing plant with nutrition until its true leaves appear (the third and fourth leaves to develop) and it's time to fertilize. Sterile seed-starting mixes provide no nutrients, so after true leaves appear, feed your seedlings weekly (and weakly) with a liquid kelp/fish emulsion combo (or add kelp one week and fish the next). If you added a little compost or some worm castings to your seed-starting mix, you can skip this step.

At this stage, you need to make tough decisions about what to do with all those little seedlings. They need breathing room for both roots and shoots, and keeping them tightly packed together means none of them will thrive. So you must thin them out, cutting off the weakest at soil level. Aim to leave only one seedling per 3-in. pot; two in larger containers. Consider this your first harvest: most seedlings are delicious in a salad.

In outdoor gardens, thin seedlings in stages. If you thin to final spacing too early, you may wind up with fewer plants than intended; bugs and slugs can make suppers out of the remaining tender starts.

How to Sow Seeds

MATERIALS

Seeds
Organic soil mix
Container(s) if planting indoors
Watering can with fine rose nozzle
Chopstick or pencil
Trowel

1 Moisten the soil before you sow. It should be damp but not wet—like a wrung-out sponge. This applies to outdoor (direct) sowing, too.

2 Fill your container(s) with soil mix. Tamp it down gently, leaving ½ in. or so of space at the top.

3 Check the seed packet for information on how deep to sow the seeds. As a rule of thumb, seeds can be planted at a depth of about twice their diameter; thus, large seeds such as beans will be sown deeper than miniscule carrot seeds. It is better to err on the side of planting too shallow; plant too deep and the seedling won't be able to reach the soil surface.

4 If you are sowing larger seeds in containers, poke a hole into the soil using a chopstick or pencil, place one seed in, and cover it with soil. For smaller seeds, sprinkle them on top and scratch them in. Depending on the size of your container, you might plant two to six seeds. Planting extra provides a fallback in case one or more fails to germinate. If you are sowing outdoors, create a shallow trench with the edge of your trowel, then scatter or place seeds evenly along the trench. Follow the spacing directions on the seed packet. Of course, you don't have to plant in straight lines. Blocks or natural-looking drifts also work.

5 Label your containers or rows if you are sowing more than one type of seed.

6 Place the containers in a warm, bright area, and wait. (If you cover your trays with a clear dome or plastic bag, you may not even need to water again until the seeds germinate. When they do, remove the bag or dome.) Some seeds germinate in days; others take weeks.

7 Set your seed trays on top of the fridge, on a sunny window ledge, or on a warm oven. You can move the trays after the seeds have germinated—although some plants, such as peppers, prefer extra warmth even after they have sprouted.

8 Keep sown soil moist (not waterlogged) throughout germination and sprouting.

Hardening Off

Your indoor seedlings have had a pretty sheltered upbringing. To put them directly outdoors without preparation would be like us getting dropped in Antarctica without a jacket. Seedlings started indoors need to go through a regimen called hardening off before being planted outside.

Hardening off involves setting your pots of seedlings outdoors for increasingly longer periods of time to get them accustomed to the elements. Start by setting them in the shade—direct sun would be more than they could take—for about an hour. During the next several days, repeat this little field trip, slowly lengthening their outdoor visits, but bringing them back indoors for the night.

Remove overcrowded seedlings as they grow, eventually thinning to the spacing distance recommended on the seed packet.

You will also start introducing them to sun, and eventually (after a week or so), you can leave them out overnight. Feel free to skip a day if the weather is particularly brutal. Cold frames, like mini greenhouses, allow you to skip all this schlepping inside and out. Just plunk your plants into the cold frame for two weeks, opening the lid for longer and longer periods of time each day.

Transplanting

After being hardened off, seedlings are ready for more permanent digs. Whether you are planting them in the ground or in a larger container, it's great to see your babies planted in their forever homes (even if you do end up eating them after a few weeks).

Dig the planting hole slightly deeper and about twice as wide as the plant pot. Unless you have already amended your soil with compost or a complete organic fertilizer, do this now, before adding the plant.

Squeeze the sides of your pot to release the plant (unless you have sown your seeds in a newspaper pot, in which case you can plant the whole package). You may need to tap the rim gently. Try not to handle the seedling. If you must, hold it by its leaves—ideally, by its seed leaves, if it still has them—never by the stem.

Test the size of the planting hole prior to removing the plant from its pot.

Never pull the plant out of its pot by its stem or leaves; instead, squeeze the sides of the pot to release the roots and let it slide out.

Place the seedling in its hole, making sure its soil is level with the surrounding soil. Do not bury the stem, except in certain cases, such as tomatoes, which benefit from being planted deeply. Gently fill in the remainder of the hole with soil, and water well. That's it!

Gently lower the transplant into the hole; it should sit at the same soil level it was in its pot.

Plant bare-root apple trees during the dormant winter months.

Planting Bare-Root Trees or Shrubs in Containers

Trees and shrubs are often sold as bare-root stock, which is exactly what it sounds like: the roots are bare, with no soil around them. Understandably, bare-root stock is sold in the winter months when the plants are dormant—an ideal time for transplanting into containers.

MATERIALS

Bare-root tree or shrub
Container slightly more than twice the size of
    plant's root system
Potting soil
Balanced, granular organic fertilizer
Trowel or small spade
Water

1 Soak the roots overnight prior to planting.

2 Thoroughly combine potting soil and fertilizer according to package directions. Add to
the container, creating a hole about twice the
size of the root system, and then mounding
some soil back into the center of the hole.

3 Spread the tree or shrub's roots out over the
mound. If you're planting a grafted tree such
as a dwarf apple, make sure that the graft
union (the bulge where the rootstock meets
the trunk) will be 2 to 3 in. above the soil line.

4 Fill the hole with loose soil, pressing it down
with your hands as you go.

5 Water well. Many young trees benefit from
staking at the time of planting.

Keeping Plants Healthy

After you have sown your seeds and planted your crops, you can move into defense mode. Your newly planted seedlings are like candy to all sorts of insects, and a weed needs no better invitation than a freshly tilled bed. But although weeds, pests, and diseases are all part of gardening, you don't have to resign yourself to losing half your crop or using chemicals to combat annoyances. The fact that you're working in a limited space—perhaps on a balcony or up off the ground in raised beds— is a leg up in the battle against garden troublemakers.

◄ Provide climbing vines like grapes the support they need. They'll stay healthy and productive, and add vertical interest.

Repeat this mantra: healthy gardens start with healthy soil. And healthy gardens are better able to withstand pests and disease. This is one of the most important lessons of organic gardening—embrace it and put it into practice.

Soil management is just the beginning. Practicing good garden maintenance techniques will also go a long way toward growing thriving crops. Similarly, preventing pests and disease and knowing how to deal with emerging weeds is more effective than grappling with these problems after they have taken hold. In this chapter, you will learn how to prevent and treat the problems that inevitably spring up right along with your seedlings.

Garden Maintenance

Maintenance encompasses all the usual suspects: weeding, watering, pruning, and basic chores. These tasks can be highly enjoyable—or a huge pain—depending on your outlook, your tools, and your setup. Get the last two right, and your outlook might change dramatically.

Essential tools

At any garden center, you can be easily suckered in by the fascinating array of tools and supplies and ornaments. But what do you actually need? One of the benefits of a small garden is that you don't need that much to take care of it. You don't need a wheelbarrow. You won't need power equipment. You may even be able to get away with a trowel instead of a shovel. For my money, a few tools are the bare essentials.

- **Trowel** for preparing small planting holes for transplants and for scooping soil into containers. Basic.

- **Hand cultivator or hoe** for loosening soil and preparing the ground for planting. These can be three-pronged forks, pared-down versions of the familiar

Try to keep a sense of humor about garden pests and accept the fact that you might end up sharing some of your harvest with them.

long-handled hoe, or designs that combine the best of both.

- **Stakes** for supporting vine tomatoes and climbers such as beans, peas, and squashes. Bamboo stakes are nice looking, while heavy-duty plastic or metal is longer lasting; found twigs and branches are a funky budget option.

- **Twine** for lashing stakes together into teepees or providing beans with something to climb.

- **Watering can or hose** for watering, obviously. Make sure you get a variable-setting nozzle for your hose or a watering can with a rose (the attachment with tiny holes on the end of the spout). Self-coiling spiral hoses are a great small-space option.

- **Pruning shears** for cutting back branches and harvesting. Good-quality pruning shears (also known as pruners or secateurs) are a must if you plan to grow any sort of woody plant, such as a fruit tree or berry shrub. But they also come in handy for pruning vining tomato plants, harvesting thick-stemmed vegetables such as cabbages, or cutting woody herbs such as rosemary.

A trowel is a small-space garden essential.

A watering can with a large rose is especially good for seedlings, because it lightly showers the plants, rather than overwhelming a small plant with a flood of water.

KEEPING PLANTS HEALTHY

- **Gloves** for protecting your hands. Gloves are not strictly necessary but are nice to have for mucky or prickly jobs—turning the compost, for example. Many types of gloves are available, from breathable (but not prickle-proof) cloth to heavy-duty rubber or leather. The best combine fabric with rubber or leather, providing breathability and protection.

Watering

Because watering is pretty much a constant task, consider spending time and money to make it an easy one. I once abandoned a small container garden on my balcony because it had no nearby water access. After the warm weather hit, I had to lug watering can after watering can up a flight of stairs, sometimes twice a day. I am a dedicated gardener, but that was just nuts.

Don't set yourself up to fail: plan out your watering strategy in advance. Make sure a hose, tap, or water barrel is easy to access and close to the garden site. Get a large, lightweight watering can to reduce your trips to the tap (and strain on your back).

Even better, remove yourself from the picture; set up a drip or low-flow automatic watering system on a timer. This requires more work and cost at the beginning, but it will pay off when you want to go away on a summer weekend and none of your friends can come by and water your plants.

How to water

Three basic rules apply when it comes to watering.

Water the soil, not the leaves. Water that collects on a plant's leaves can promote disease, especially on the leaves of potatoes, tomatoes, squash, and melons.

Water that sits on a plant's leaves can invite disease. You can't do much about the rain, but you can avoid using overhead sprinklers or indiscriminate use of the spray nozzle.

After you fill the reservoir in a self-watering container, the plant will have access to water for several days.

Make Your Watering More Efficient

Amend your soil. Add compost, manure, or other organic matter, and it will hold water like a sponge. (Be careful not to add too much organic matter to container soil or it can become compacted.)

Mulch. Layer on compost, pebbles, bark, leaf mold, straw, or newspaper, which will act like a blanket on the soil, reducing evaporation.

Use large containers. The smaller the pot, the more frequently you have to water. Remember that terra-cotta containers lose water quickly.

Use self-watering containers. Self-watering pots have a reservoir in the bottom that you fill once a week or less, depending on the size of the reservoir. Most types act by wicking water up through the potting mix, providing a steady source of water to roots. Ready-made self-watering containers are often pricey but you can make your own. (Search online for "self-watering containers.")

Use a soaker hose or drip irrigation. Both options are great for slowly soaking the soil. A soaker hose is perforated with tiny holes all along its length; lay one in your garden bed and it will deliver water directly to each plant. Drip irrigation systems use a main hose to deliver water to multiple drippers or sprayers, which can be positioned at regular intervals or custom designed to reach each plant or container. These systems can stay in place year-round if properly winterized and can also be put on a timer for completely effortless watering.

Water in the morning. Watering early allows plants to absorb water before the sun gets high and the air heats up, providing your plants with fuel to withstand the heat of the day. Watering in the morning also allows plenty of time for any water to evaporate from leaves, which reduces the possibility of fungal diseases encouraged by cooler nighttime temperatures. Second best is watering in the evening; least desirable is at midday.

Water deeply, not more frequently. Better to soak plants infrequently, allowing water to penetrate thoroughly, than to lightly sprinkle the surface every day. Plants' roots go where the water is. If you water deeply, roots will grow deep into the soil, anchoring plants and helping them withstand drought and winds.

Several signs can indicate that a plant needs water, such as soil that is pulled away from the sides of a container, and plants with limp, floppy leaves. Before you let them get that far, try a variation on the cake-readiness test. Stick your finger into the soil past the first knuckle. If the soil feels dry and doesn't stick to your finger when you pull it out, add water. Small containers can be checked by lifting them up; you'll soon get a feel for how heavy they should be when wet enough.

How often to water depends on a number of factors. Young seedlings and transplants require more frequent watering than do established plants and trees. All plants require extra watering in hot weather. Sandy soils offer great drainage, but need regular replenishing. And container gardens need watering more often than inground gardens.

Staking and Trellising

Small-space gardeners just don't have the real estate to let vegetable plants sprawl across the ground. Staking plants—training them or supporting them to grow upward—saves space, prevents disease, and makes vegetables easier to harvest. Peas, pole beans, cucumbers, squash, melon, vining (indeterminate) tomatoes, kiwi, raspberries, blackberries, and grapes are all good candidates for vertical growing.

Install your trellis or stakes before or at planting time to avoid damaging roots later on. Train plants to climb by wrapping their tendrils around the stakes (in the case of peas and beans) or by tying their shoots to supports as they grow (cut up old pantyhose or soft rags to use as ties).

A teepee or obelisk can make a great garden focal point and can support a number of vertical growers such as peas and pole beans. You can make your own out of bamboo stakes, sticks, metal poles, or lumber lashed together at the top.

A square or rectangular grid leaning against a wall can be used to support any climbing fruits and vegetables, especially heavier ones such as melons and squashes. Make your own out of wood, or look for old wrought iron gates or headboards.

Arbors and other overhead structures are perfect for supporting kiwis and grapes. They can do double duty as shade providers for you or for cool-season crops such as salad greens.

Tree stakes, which are thicker and taller than general-purpose garden stakes, can be used to support dwarf fruit trees and prevent them from breaking or leaning when weighed down with fruit.

Wires are great for keeping blackberries and raspberries contained. If berries are grown along a fence, their sprawling branches can be supported by running a wire along the length of the patch and securing both ends to the fence. In a free-standing patch, wooden posts with horizontal crossbars threaded with wire running on either side of the plants will corral them and keep them manageable. Clear fishing line is a good option if you would rather not see the supports; plastic-guarded clothesline wire also works well.

Pruning

Most annual vegetables require little if any pruning in the true sense of the word (indeterminate tomatoes are a notable exception). But even if you are not growing vines, shrubs, or trees, you should understand how pruning can help your plants. Pruning removes dead, dying, or diseased growth; improves air circulation; allows sunlight to reach and ripen fruits; and improves or controls the size and shape of a plant.

Prune a tree or plant to influence its shape and size.

Cucumbers grow vertically on a copper-supported trellis, freeing up garden space.

Pinching out

Pinching out—regularly removing the tips of a plant's new growth using your thumb and forefinger—causes the plant to produce side shoots, becoming bushier and more vigorous in the process. This old practice forces the plant to produce new growth, increasing the harvest. Most vegetables do not need to be pruned this way, but many herbs do.

Herbs want nothing more than to produce flowers and seed, continuing their genetic line. But for our (culinary) purposes, we want leaves, not flowers, so we pinch out the strongest new growth to prevent the plant from flowering. Many herbs benefit from being pinched back early and often, starting when young plants have produced four sets of true leaves.

Pruning tomatoes

Indeterminate, or vining, tomatoes should be pruned to keep them from becoming unwieldy beasts. Determinate, or bush, tomatoes do not need pruning; the seed packet or plant label should tell you which type you have. To prune indeterminate types, pinch out the shoots that develop between the main stem and its leaf branches. If these are left to grow, each of the shoots—called suckers—will

Suckers develop on tomato stems from the elbow between the main stem and leaf branch.

Pinch out suckers with your thumb and forefinger.

develop into an offshoot the size of the main stem; the plant will produce more fruit if you remove these suckers. You can also selectively remove any stems not bearing fruit (including flower trusses) at the end of summer to force the plant to put its energy into ripening existing fruits.

Pruning berry shrubs

Blueberry and cranberry bushes should be pruned in late winter or early spring, before new growth starts. Annual pruning encourages good fruit production. During the first year, strip off any flower buds to force the plant to

Your tomato will be more productive after the suckers are removed.

put energy into root development. During the first couple of years, prune only the dead, damaged, and diseased branches. Starting in the third year, prune out crossing branches to allow light to penetrate into the center of the shrub. Prune back the tips of vigorous branches to encourage bushy growth. Starting in the fifth year, cut back two of the oldest branches to the ground each year to encourage new growth. The best fruit is produced on second- and third-year branches.

Pruning cane fruits

Raspberries and blackberries can be pruned in autumn. Just remove all the canes that produced fruit that summer; cane fruits produce berries on year-old growth. You can also prune canes that have outgrown their space; cut them back to restrict their growth.

Pruning fruit trees

Fruit trees are usually pruned to create good shape, and the shape that is right for your tree is usually determined by its type. Columnar trees, which grow to a maximum of 10 ft. tall but only 2 ft. wide, are easily maintained by pruning side branches to the third leaf bud. Dwarf or semi-dwarf trees can be espaliered (trained to lie flat and often grown against a fence or wall) or pruned to create a vase-shaped open center, which allows sunlight and air to reach the center of the tree.

With all types of pruning, think about how you want the tree to look several years from now, and keep that in mind as you make your cuts. When removing limbs, make the cut parallel to the trunk and slightly in front of the limb's collar, which is the wrinkled area where the limb and tree trunk join together. When you prune branch tips, make diagonal cuts about ¼ in. or so above a bud that faces out in the direction you want it to grow. Be careful not to prune out any fruiting spurs—short, gnarly branches that produce fruit. Pruning apples and pears is best done when the tree is dormant, in late winter or early spring

KEEPING PLANTS HEALTHY

before trees begin to bud; however, if you want to reduce the overall size of the tree, prune in summer. Stone fruits such as apricots, cherries, and peaches should be pruned after flowering in spring.

To prune a tree into an open center shape, select four to six horizontal branches spaced evenly around the tree. They should be no more than 5 ft. from the ground (lower is fine, too). These will form your vase shape and will serve as the main fruit producers. Next, cut back the main leader, or trunk, at an angle and just above the highest of your selected horizontal branches. This creates the open center. If your tree is young and does not have many horizontal branches, you can prune the trunk where you would like branches to grow (2 to 3 ft. from the ground is suggested). New branches will grow just below this cut.

Fruit trees can also be espaliered, a method of pruning and training them into simple or elaborate patterns. Espaliered trees are especially popular for small gardens because they are trained flat and take up little space, yet they produce abundantly. Apples, apricots, figs, peaches, pears, plums, and nectarines are all good candidates for espalier.

"Cordon" is a word used to describe growth trained in a line, on a single or double branch. Cordon is often associated with espalier. The horizontal cordon is a popular and relatively easy espalier shape to create. An apple

This tree has been trained into a horizontal cordon, a popular espalier design.

or pear tree in this shape can be grown along a wall or fence. (Once established, it can actually become a fence.) To train a tree into this shape, choose two lower branches as the lowest tier, or cordon. Loosely tie these branches to a horizontal support such as wires or a trellis, gradually tightening them over the following months until they are fully horizontal. Repeat with two or three sets of horizontal branches above this lowest cordon. Or, if the tree lacks suitable branches, cut the leader back to the lowest support. New growth will form at the pruning site, and you can begin to shape it to suit your will. After the tree has achieved the shape you want, regularly snip off errant growth to maintain the shape.

To prune branch tips of a fruit tree, make diagonal cuts about ¼ in. above a bud that faces out in the direction you want it to grow.

Weeds

One of the great things about having a small garden is that weeds are few. In containers, they may even be nonexistent. Weeds can be troublesome—even downright nasty—in an inground garden, however. Philosophical types might argue that a weed is just a plant in the wrong place, but weeds compete with crops for nutrients and space and can take over your garden if you fail to keep them at bay.

But they can also be helpful. Many weeds accumulate nutrients in their leaves, which can be harvested to add goodness to your compost. Others make a tasty addition to salads or sautés.

Without using chemical herbicides, you can control weeds in a number of ways using items you have around the house. Not all types of weeds will respond to one particular tactic; the best successes often result from a combination of methods.

Hand weeding

Hand weeding is a simple concept—yank out that plant! But not all weeds are so compliant. Many have deep taproots (such as dandelion) or extensive root systems (such as bindweed). These need to be dug out carefully, and you must make sure that you remove the entire root. Annual weeds are easily removed with a hoe or cultivator; the key is to get them before they flower and set seed. Most weeds are easiest to remove when they are small and the soil is damp.

You can turn some weeds into food for the plants you do want in your garden by adding them to your compost. Compost only the leaves. Exclude flowers, seed heads, and the roots of perennial weeds or they will spread throughout your compost.

Mulching to suppress weeds

Mulch is magic when it comes to weed control. Spreading organic mulch such as straw, leaf mold, or compost

KEEPING PLANTS HEALTHY

across the soil surface in a layer 2 to 4 in. thick will suppress weed growth, especially in combination with hand weeding. Do this regularly (at least twice a year), and you may never see weeds again. For really beastly weeds such as Japanese knotweed, a cover of thick plastic or old carpet is your best bet (cover this with mulch or build raised beds on top).

To create a new garden bed on top of soil that has been colonized by weeds, sheet mulching is an excellent solution. Smother the weeds with layers of cardboard, leaves, and manure, and let the worms turn it all into rich garden soil.

Other organic weed controls

If mulching and hand weeding are not working for you, you might consider a home-brewed herbicide. Many organic gardeners swear by a mixture of salt and vinegar—awesome on chips, deadly for weeds. Mix up a solution of 16 parts vinegar to 1 part salt, add a squirt of dish soap, and spray this onto weed leaves. It won't discriminate between crabgrass and collard greens—it will kill both—so apply it carefully. Avoid using it too close to vegetables, because the salts can disperse in the soil and kill the good plants. Salt and vinegar kill leaves on contact, but the weed's

Planting in rows makes weeds easy to identify and remove.

When the soil is damp, weeds are easier to remove.

roots may survive and resprout. For perennial weeds, you may need to douse the plant with this solution to kill the roots.

Drench weeds that pop up between pavers and patio tiles with boiling water. Like vinegar, hot water is indiscriminate; avoid using this technique near plants you want to live.

Pests

Unfortunately, you are not the only one looking forward to tasting your homegrown fruits and veggies. No matter where you live, pests seem to find your plants—even on a rooftop balcony. Having bugs mow down a fresh crop of veggies is infuriating, and it is natural to react with an unnatural defense. But pesticides shouldn't be your first line of attack.

Most chemical pesticides are toxic not only to the pests they target, but also to curious children, pets, wildlife, and other innocent bystanders. These toxins also have a long-term detrimental effect on human and environmental health, which is why they are increasingly being banned from home use.

But even organic pesticides have their problems. Many kill the good bugs along with the bad. And although it might not seem like it, most insects are beneficial (or at least benign) in the garden. Although blasting those cursed aphids with home-brewed insecticidal soap might seem like a good idea, look before you spray. Perhaps some beneficial bugs are already on the case.

Focus on maintaining healthy soil, rotating your crops, starting with clean pots and tools, and choosing disease-resistant edibles if you are concerned about pests. Finally, let companion plants do some of the work!

Support Workers

Some insects and animals pollinate your crops and help control destructive bugs. Attract these garden helpers by interplanting herbs and flowers they love amongst your crops.

Pest predators	minute pirate bugs	hummingbirds	clover
aphid midges	praying mantids	tachinid flies	currant
assassin bugs	rove beetles	moths	dill
bats	soldier beetles	wasps	echinacea
big-eyed bugs	spiders		honeysuckle
birds	wasps	**Plants to attract**	lavender
centipedes		**the good guys**	phlox
damsel bugs	**Common garden**	anise hyssop	sedum
frogs and toads	**pollinators**	aster	sweet alyssum
ground beetles	bees	basil	yarrow
hoverflies	beetles	bee balm	
lacewings	butterflies	borage	
ladybugs	hoverflies	calendula or pot marigold	

Companion Planting to Help and Hinder

Companion planting is a classic organic gardening technique that involves matching plants that help each other. Plant companions can repel insects or attract pollinators, supply nitrogen, provide shade, or act as vertical support.

Some North American indigenous groups mastered this technique with the traditional "three sisters" grouping of corn, beans, and squash. Beans supply nitrogen to the corn and squash; corn stalks provide vertical support to climbing beans; and squash shades the soil, retaining moisture, while its prickly vines discourage squirrels and raccoons from accessing tender corn cobs. You can put the same symbiosis to work in your garden, whether it's fighting pests or lending plants a hand.

Bees and other pollinators are important forces in the garden.

Plants that repel pests

Many strongly scented herbs and vegetables are repellent to insect pests. Chives, garlic, shallots, onions, and leeks help to repel slugs, snails, aphids, white flies, carrot rust flies, cabbage worms, and even some rodents. Plant them among carrots, broccoli, cauliflower, and other pest-prone plants. Basil, dill, fennel, marigold, mint, and sage look pretty and also keep pests at bay.

Organic insect control

Heavy pest infestations can require intervention. Insects go after weaklings; the best thing may be to destroy the infested plant. The next least invasive approach is to trap or remove by hand larger pests such as slugs and caterpillars. Use a strong jet of water to knock aphids and other soft-bodied insects off leaves. Repeat daily. If none of this is working, consider a few products or techniques.

SPRAYS AND POWDERS Although these products are not highly toxic to humans and other mammals, when applying them wear a mask, a long-sleeved shirt, and long pants for protection.

Ladybugs are an organic gardener's best friend.

Aphids will flock to nasturtiums, edible flowers commonly used to lure pests away from other plants.

Borage is a large, pretty plant with delicate, cucumber-flavored, edible flowers. It attracts predatory insects and honeybees.

Marigolds, here interplanted with amaranth, are a classic choice for planting with edibles. Their distinctive scent is repellent to many pest insects.

Biological control. *Bacillus thuringiensis*, or Bt for short, is a naturally occurring bacterium. Applied as a liquid spray or powder, Bt must be ingested by the insect. Be sure to choose the variety that will target your specific pest. Use Bt as a last resort; butterfly larvae are affected by its application.

Homemade sprays. The trouble with these is that most kill both good and bad insects and can harm plants if improperly prepared or applied. Most recipes call for various combinations of dish soap, garlic, citrus, or hot peppers.

Horticultural oils. Primarily used to control pests on fruit and nut trees and cane fruits. Spraying while the plant is dormant can help destroy overwintering insects. Follow package directions carefully.

Insecticidal soap. Kills soft-bodied insects such as aphids, whiteflies, mites, and mealybugs on contact, which means you have to spray the actual insect. Safe for the environment, but can also kill beneficial insects.

Neem. Derived from the seed of the neem tree, which has natural insecticidal properties. Kills a range of pests including aphids, cabbage loopers, leaf miners, and whiteflies. Also controls fungal diseases.

BARRIERS AND TRAPS These can work effectively on some pests, and they are less disruptive than insecticides.

Fruit bags. Slip paper bags over developing apples and pears. Secure the bag with twine and remove just before harvest.

Insecticidal soap is safe for the environment, but it will kill good bugs as well as bad.

Beer traps. Take advantage of slugs' weakness for beer. Bury a tuna can until the lip is level with the soil. Half fill it with beer. Slugs climb in and drown—not a bad way to go, all things considered.

Copper. Gives slugs and snails an electric shock on contact. Form a copper ring around each plant, or the entire bed.

Abrasives. Discourage slugs and snails, sowbugs, earwigs, and caterpillars by spreading a 2-in.-wide barrier of wood ash, sawdust, crushed eggshells, or seashells around your plants. These sharp-edged materials irritate the coatings of soft-bodied insects.

Collars. Cut tubes from toilet paper or paper towel rolls into 3-in. sections, place the tubes over the seedlings, and push them halfway into the soil.

Floating row covers. Drape a sheet of sheer fabric or plastic over your crops to control many pests, including carrot rust flies, caterpillars, leafhoppers, and Colorado potato beetles. Remove covers after plants are sturdy, and to allow crop pollination.

Sticky traps. Dozens of these types of traps are available. Keep in mind that they are nonselective and also trap beneficial insects.

Trap crops. These plants attract insect pests away from your primary food crop, then can be destroyed after infestation. Nasturtiums and broad beans attract aphids, mustard draws cabbage worms, and chervil lures slugs.

Common insect pests and ways to thwart them

Every year, it seems I encounter a new insect foe. Several of the most common garden pests, including some of my personal nemeses, are listed here.

Aphids. These tiny, pear-shaped, soft-bodied insects can be green, gray, black, or pink. Aphids secrete sticky honeydew excrement that covers infested plants, attracting ants and black mold. Aphids suck the sap from plants, especially favoring tender new growth. Affected leaves

A sticky trap helps protect container peppers from unwanted visitors.

KEEPING PLANTS HEALTHY

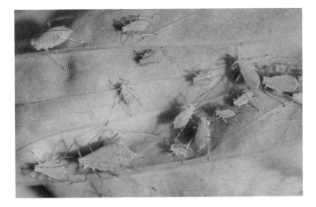

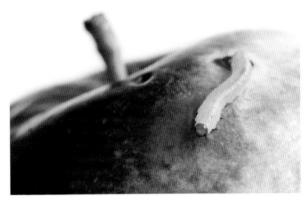

Apple maggots. These white maggots tunnel through apples, blueberries, and plums, and can be controlled by regularly collecting dropped fruit, hanging traps in trees during the growing season, bagging fruit, and attracting predatory ground beetles.

Aphids, continued

and stems become twisted and weak. Knock them off with a strong jet of water; attract or buy ladybugs, lacewings, or aphid midges; or spray with insecticidal soap. The key to victory is consistent (daily) effort.

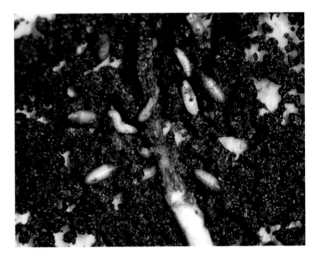

Cabbage maggots. Small white larvae tunnel into the roots of broccoli, cabbage, radishes, and turnips, stunting or killing the plants. Use floating row covers to prevent adults from laying eggs.

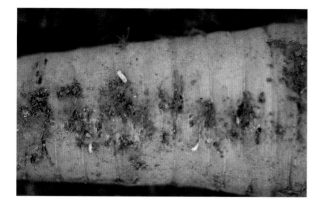

Carrot rust flies. These flies are attracted to young carrots, but they can also infest plants like parsnips and celery. Little white maggots tunnel into roots, stunting or killing the plant. Practice crop rotation; use floating row covers before seedlings emerge (and leave them covered until harvest); plant resistant cultivars such as the 'Flyaway' carrot; and interplant your carrots with garlic, leeks, or onions.

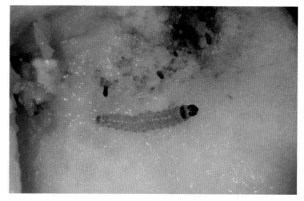

Codling moth. A fruit tree pest that affects stone and pome fruits, most commonly the apple. Its larvae tunnel into the fruit, spoiling it. Spray the tree with horticultural oil, bag developing fruit, buy and release parasitic wasps, and use sticky tree bands to trap the larvae as they climb up the trunk.

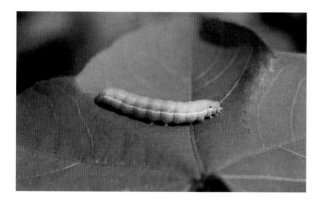

Caterpillars. In their larval (caterpillar) stage, armyworms, cabbage loopers, imported cabbage worms, cankerworms, leaf rollers, and tomato hornworms can destroy your garden—and your will to live. Hand pick caterpillars daily, attract or release parasitic wasps, cover plants with floating row covers, and spray the plants with Bt as a last resort. Spray fruit trees with horticultural oil.

Colorado potato beetle. This yellow-and-black-striped beetle and its larvae prey on potatoes and tomatoes, among other crops, feeding on the leaves. Lay a cloth or newspaper under the infested crops and shake the plant to remove bugs (best done in the early morning when they are groggy). Use mulch to attract ground beetle predators, spray infested plants with neem, and use floating row covers.

KEEPING PLANTS HEALTHY

Cucumber beetles. Striped or spotted cucumber beetles feed on the leaves and roots of corn and squash plants, and of course, cucumbers. Shake them off plants as you would Colorado potato beetles, or use floating row covers (and hand-pollinate the flowers).

Flea beetles. These tiny black or brown beetles get their name from their jumping habit, similar to that of fleas. They riddle the leaves of vegetable crops with little holes, sometimes killing seedlings. Use floating row covers, spray with neem, and create shady conditions (flea beetles are sun worshippers).

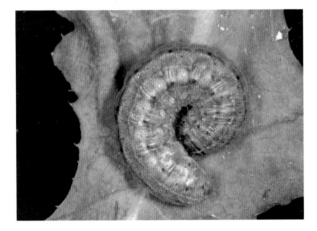

Cutworms. Cutworm caterpillars emerge at night to feed on the stems of seedlings at the soil line, cutting stems in two. Use collars and attract predatory ground beetles by providing permanent plantings, mulch, and groundcovers.

Leafhoppers. Tiny, wedge-shaped insects that spring like grasshoppers when disturbed. They suck sap from plants, causing leaves to curl and yellow. Attract parasitic wasps or spray with insecticidal soap or neem.

Mealybugs. Small, oval, soft-bodied insects covered in white, waxy fluff that leave honeydew excrement behind. Knock them off with a strong jet of water, introduce mealybug destroyer larvae, or spray them with insecticidal soap.

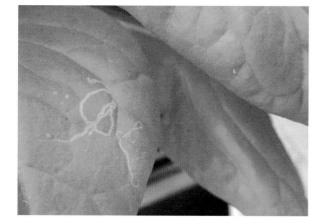

Leaf miners. Hard-to-see larvae leave pale "scribbles" on leafy greens; destroy these leaves. As a last resort, spray the plant with neem.

Mexican bean beetles. With their black spots, these pale orange, oval beetles look similar to ladybugs. They feed on plants from the legume family, skeletonizing the leaves. Use floating row covers, release or attract predatory or parasitic insects, or spray with neem.

Nematodes. Some of these microscopic worms are helpful and are sold to control pest insects. Others are harmful plant parasites, causing damage to stems, leaves, and particularly root vegetables. Practice crop rotation, and plant a cover crop of marigolds, which suppresses the microscopic worms.

Mites. Most are nearly invisible to the naked eye, including the common spider mite. Damage appears on the undersides of leaves as a speckling of light dots. If mites are not controlled, leaves will turn yellow or bronze and drop. Fine webbing may be visible in heavy infestations. To control, attract beneficial insects such as lacewings and minute pirate bugs, spray the undersides of leaves with a strong jet of water, or spray the plant with insecticidal soap or neem. Spray fruit trees with horticultural oil.

Plum curculios. These warty-looking beetles lay eggs inside the fruits of apple, apricot, cherry, peach, and of course, plum trees. Infested fruit, which usually drops prematurely, shows a crescent moon–shaped scar in the flesh. Spread a sheet beneath the tree and shake or jar the pests onto the sheet; collect and destroy them.

Squash vine borers. Narrow red and brown moths produce larvae that bore into the vines of squash plants, causing vines to wilt or die. Use floating row covers (do the pollinating yourself or remove the covers later in the season).

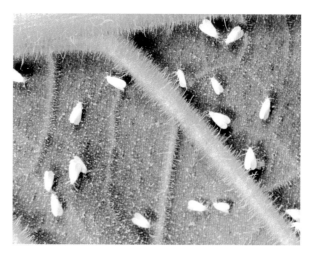

Slugs and snails. Munching on seedlings and leaves, these pests leave their telltale trail of slime. Set up barriers such as copper strips or abrasives, set out beer traps, hand pick the critters on rainy days or in the early morning when they are out and about, and encourage predatory ground beetles.

Whiteflies. Tiny whiteflies congregate on the undersides of leaves. Like aphids and mealybugs, they secrete honeydew, which promotes the growth of mold. Use sticky traps, attract predators and parasites such as ground beetles and wasps, and spray them with insecticidal soap or neem.

Wireworms. The larvae of the click beetle, which, when turned on its back, produces an audible click as it rights itself. Carrots and potatoes are favorites of the wireworm, which bores into roots or tubers. Garden beds that replace lawn are particularly susceptible, since wireworms hang out in sod. Cultivate the soil deeply to destroy larvae, or sink chunks of potato into soil where wireworms are active; they will be attracted to the potatoes, which can be collected and destroyed.

Other pests

Insects are not the only pests that can dampen your gardening spirits. If you grow food, you are sure to meet your local wildlife.

Small mammals such as squirrels, rats, and raccoons love to get their paws on fresh produce. Grow squash and prickly berries as a barrier around corn, tomatoes, and other favorites, or surround containers with a chicken wire cage. Line the inside of raised beds with hardware cloth to fend off gophers and other tunnelers.

Cats and dogs can also be pests. Cultivated soil is a fresh litter box to a cat; cover freshly seeded beds with chicken wire until plants are larger, or invest in an electronic device that uses sound or water spray to frighten intruders. Dogs can trample and pee on plants; a low fence will discourage them.

Birds are welcome garden guests—until they eat your crops. Protect plants by covering them with netting or cages, scare birds off by hanging reflectors or noise-makers, or by setting out plastic predators. Switch tactics frequently.

Humans also cause their share of garden damage. Many people have no qualms about stealing your ripe tomatoes or walking through your beds. A low fence can help reinforce boundaries; also try planting easy-to-steal edibles at the back of the bed. Children, especially toddlers, can also be a force of destruction. When she was younger, my daughter loved to pluck unripe tomatoes, upend containers, and throw handfuls of dirt. Other than developing a level of tolerance for chaos, my strategy was to distract her with her own bucketful of dirt and a shovel. I did larger garden tasks during her nap time.

Diseases

If it's not mites, it's mildew. Fortunately, many common plant diseases are relatively easy to prevent, or at least control, using good practices. Crop rotation, cleaning up leaf and plant debris, destroying (not composting) diseased plant matter, watering effectively, choosing disease-resistant plants, fertilizing properly, and pruning to promote good health all go a long way to prevent the spread of disease. However, despite all your efforts, sometimes disease is inevitable.

Blight. Tomatoes, potatoes and peppers are susceptible to both early and late blight, fungal diseases that cause dark spots on leaves and eventually stems. Both types can overwinter in the soil, so avoid planting these crops in the same place year after year. Late blight thrives in cool, damp weather; prevent it by avoiding overhead watering (move or plant tomatoes under cover to avoid direct rainfall). Destroy infected plants, and do not compost them.

Bacterial canker. Bacterial canker affects fruits such as apricot, cherry, peach, and plum, causing branches to wilt and die. Oozing lesions on the branches emit a red, sour-smelling gum. Prune off infected branches, sterilizing pruning shears between cuts with a quick dip in a 1:2 hydrogen peroxide and water bath to prevent the spread of the disease.

Blossom end rot. A dark, rotten-looking spot on the bottom of a tomato or pepper plant means blossom end rot. It signals a calcium deficiency, often caused by erratic watering. Keep soil evenly moist.

Brown rot. Apricots, cherries, peaches, and plums are susceptible, especially in humid areas. This fungal disease can cause blossoms to die and creates brown spots on fruit, eventually destroying it. Remove and destroy damaged fruit and any branches showing lesions. Sulfur or copper sprays also help.

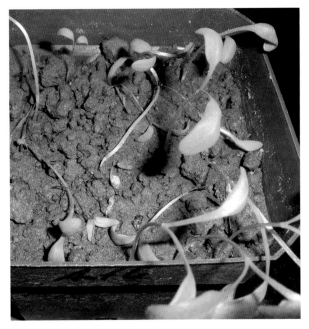

Damping-off. New seedlings can be attacked by this fungus, causing plants to keel over at soil level. The plant's lower stems usually appear thin and dark, as if crushed or rotting. Damping-off also affects seeds before they sprout. Start seeds in sterilized containers and soil, provide excellent drainage and air circulation, and do not overwater.

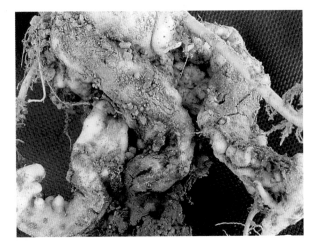

Clubroot. This fungal infection causes the roots of broccoli, cabbage, kale, turnips, and other crops to swell and become twisted, preventing them from absorbing water. Affected plants appear stunted or wilted. Unfortunately, clubroot lingers in the soil; do not replant the same plants in an infected spot for several years. Add lime to the soil.

Fire blight. This bacterial disease affects apple and pear trees, causing leaves to blacken and growing tips to curl. If you do nothing to control fire blight, it can kill the entire tree. Prune off affected branches well below the infected areas, sterilizing pruning shears between cuts. In winter, inspect branches for cankers and prune them out.

Mildews. Downy and powdery mildews are fungal diseases that affect leaves and sometimes fruit. Downy mildew, which appears as yellow or brown spots on the tops of leaves and downy spots on the bottoms, is most prevalent in cool, damp weather. Avoid overhead watering and spray with neem. Powdery mildew looks like a dusting of flour across the leaf surface, and thrives in hot, humid weather and in shade. Squash plants are particularly susceptible. Prune out infected leaves to promote good airflow; move plants to a sunnier locale, or spray with neem.

Mosaic viruses. Mainly affecting large-leaved crops such as cucumbers and squash, mosaic viruses cause yellow or white patches on foliage and may result in misshapen fruit. Destroy infected plants. Control aphids and cucumber beetles, which spread the disease.

Rust. This fungal disease appears in the form of rust-colored spots or streaks on leaves. To control, remove and destroy infected parts; dust with sulfur to control mild cases, and practice crop rotation.

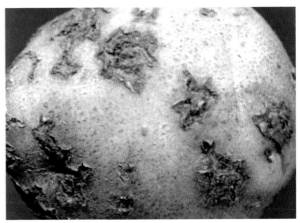

Peach leaf curl. A virus affecting peaches and nectarines, peach leaf curl causes leaves to become distorted and reddish. Infected leaves drop early, and fruit production is reduced. Choose resistant cultivars and use lime sulfur sprays.

Scab. Scab commonly affect potatoes and other root crops, as well as apples and other fruit trees, causing brown or dark green rough spots on fruit or roots. Prevent potato scab by practicing crop rotation and planting resistant selections. In fruit trees, prevent infection by cleaning up leaves and dropped fruit each fall, and spray trees with copper or sulfur. Prune to promote good air circulation, and choose resistant plants.

Wilt. Fusarium wilt and verticillium wilt cause plants to, well, wilt. Leaves turn yellow and drop, and plants may die. These fungi remain in the soil for years, making crop rotation ineffective. Fusarium wilt is common in warm temperatures, and verticillium wilt favors cool climates. Choose resistant plants, and remove and destroy infected plants.

Troubleshooting Guide

Sometimes when a plant is ailing, it's not obvious if you're dealing with a pest, a disease, or something else entirely. Here's a guide to solving the most common small-space veggie garden mysteries.

PROBLEM	POSSIBLE CAUSE	SOLUTION
Tall, spindly plants with pale leaves and low flower or fruit production	Too little sunshine; overcrowding	Move the plant or container into a sunnier location; reflect light using mirrors or light-colored walls; prune shade trees, if applicable. Alternatively, replace the plant with something more shade-tolerant. Spindly growth can also be a result of overcrowding; thin plants to ensure they have the space—and sunlight—they require.
Leaves have yellow-brown crinkled tips and edges	Too much heat and possibly not enough water	Move container plants into the shade of larger plants or containers; erect screens or a trellis to provide shade (grow beans or other climbers up them to maximize growing space); provide adequate water.
Plant is wilted (soil is dry)	Not enough water	Provide adequate water. Consider investing in drip irrigation, soaker hoses, or self-watering containers. If container-grown plants regularly dry out despite frequent watering, transplant into a larger container: the plant may be root-bound.

KEEPING PLANTS HEALTHY

Troubleshooting Guide, continued

PROBLEM	POSSIBLE CAUSE	SOLUTION
Plant is wilted (soil is very wet)	Overwatering and/or poor drainage	Overwatering is hard to avoid in containers without—or with blocked—drainage holes. Ensure your container is draining well, and raise it off the ground using planter feet (forget the saucer; those just trap water). With inground gardens, poor drainage can be resolved by building raised beds, or by amending the soil with plenty of sand and organic matter.
Damaged or ripped leaves; loss of topsoil	Wind damage	Wind damage is common in rooftop and high-rise balcony gardens. Protect your plants by erecting trellises or using hardy, dense shrubs or plants as screens. A layer of mulch will reduce moisture loss caused by winds.
Yellowing lower leaves; stunted growth	Nitrogen deficiency or overwatering	Apply a nitrogen-rich supplement such as fish emulsion, chicken manure, or cottonseed meal. Ensure good drainage and water appropriately.
Purplish leaves and leaf veins; stunted growth	Phosphorus deficiency or cool temperatures	Apply a phosphorus-rich supplement such as bone meal, rock phosphate, or greensand. If low temperatures are the suspected cause, provide warmth in the form of a cloche or row cover.
Yellowing, brown-spotted, or curling leaves	Potassium deficiency	Apply a potassium-rich supplement such as greensand, kelp, or wood ash.
Tips or edges of leaves brown and break off. Surface of soil or exterior of container shows white residue.	Salt accumulation due to chemical fertilizer use or water-softening systems	Avoid chemical fertilizers; flush excess salts from containers by thoroughly watering until water flows out the drainage hole.
Bolting: cool-season plants such as lettuce or radishes send up a tall central flowering stalk and set seed, causing the leaves or root to become bitter or overly spicy	Sudden change in temperature; too much heat	Plant cool-season crops as soon as soil can be worked in spring to allow time for plants to develop before the heat of summer hits. Succession plant every one to three weeks to improve success. Provide shade during hot weather.
Seeds not germinating	Poor or old seed; temperature too hot or too cold	Some seeds, such as parsnip, only remain viable for an average of a year. For best germination success, buy new seeds every year or two. Temperature also has an effect on germination: lettuce, for example, won't germinate during hot summer days, while beans will perish in cold soil.

PROBLEM	POSSIBLE CAUSE	SOLUTION
Plant or fruits not ready to harvest before cool weather hits	Planting a slow-to-mature variety in an area with a short growing season; starting plants too late in the season	Harvest green tomatoes and other fruits if frost is imminent and allow them to ripen indoors. Leave frost-tolerant plants in the ground: you may be able to harvest in spring. Next year, choose varieties with a low "days to maturity" number, and get a head start by buying transplants or starting seeds indoors.
Prevalence of foliar diseases such as powdery mildew	Overcrowding; improper watering techniques	Water the soil, not the leaves. Allow plants enough space and air circulation by avoiding the temptation to overcrowd. Use stakes and trellises if applicable.
Pests plague your garden	Plants are stressed due to overcrowding, under watering, overwatering, lack or excess of sunlight or heat, and/or nutrient deficiency; you've used the same soil for plants from the same family for successive years; your garden isn't attracting pest predators	Plant the right plant in the right place (i.e., sun lovers in full sun) and make sure its nutrient, water, and air circulation needs are met. Rotate your crops to protect them from soilborne pests, and sanitize your containers annually. Plant herbs and flowers that attract beneficial insects.

Making the Most of Limited Space

When you want to grow food in a small space, every square inch of soil has to work extra hard. Experienced small-space gardeners use a number of techniques to get the most from their gardens. Practicing succession planting, vertical growing, and winter gardening, for example, allow you to harvest more food over a longer season. Learn the basics, then put them into practice in your garden.

◄ A little imagination can bring an edible garden to even the most unlikely nooks and spaces.

Succession Planting

Succession planting is a technique that produces a series of crops from a single plot or container. For example, you might start early in the spring with arugula or radishes—cold-tolerant crops that mature quickly. Next you could sow main-season edibles such as beans, cucumbers, or tomatoes. Then, in late summer as these are being harvested, you could plant another cool-season crop such as endive or kale for fall or winter harvest.

The idea is to not let valuable garden space sit idle, and to be ready to plant something new whenever a space opens up. In fact, you can often interplant your new crop while still harvesting the last. Just time it so there will be enough space when the new crop starts to need more elbow room. You can also sow seeds at the same time you plant seedlings of the same type; the transplants will give you a jump on the next harvest.

The term succession planting is also used to describe planting the same edible in one- to three-week intervals, depending on how long it takes the particular type of vegetable to reach maturity. Also known as succession sowing, this technique extends the harvest period and avoids a glut of one particular crop. Fast-maturing crops are great candidates: arugula, beans, beets, carrots, lettuce and salad greens, radishes, scallions, and spinach.

Interplanting

Maximize your yields by planting together crops that grow at different rates (or root depths). For example, sow quick-growing lettuces alongside your tomato seedlings;

Interplanting a variety of complementary edibles gives this raised bed visual appeal and improved pest resistance.

you will harvest several salads before your tomatoes even start to ripen. As your tomatoes grow, they will provide shade to keep your greens from bolting in the heat. Many companion planting principles can be applied to inter-planting; don't be afraid to combine the two.

Cut-and-Come-Again Crops

When harvesting loose-leaf lettuces and other greens, just remove a few of the outer leaves; the plant will continue to produce new leaves. (Bonus: because you're just taking a few of the leaves at a time, you won't be left with an empty pot.) Some types of greens, notably mesclun, can be cut off right at the stem when they are seedlings. They will regrow, and you can repeat the process two or three times throughout the season. Arugula, Chinese cabbage, chard, chervil, chicory, collard greens, cress, dandelion, endive, escarole, kale, leaf lettuces, mizuna, and mustard are good cut-and-come-again candidates.

Vertical Gardening

While the square footage of your outdoor space may be small, you can maximize growing room by thinking creatively about how you use the vertical space available to you. Grow anything you can up stakes, teepees, trellises, or arbors—vertical gardening makes the most of valuable garden space *and* packs a great visual punch. Think of trellises or screens as living walls in your garden house—decorate with green! The usual suspects include peas, pole beans, tomatoes, berries, kiwis, and grapes, but cucumbers, squash, and melons can also be trained upward on sturdy supports.

Also consider growing not just up, but *on* your walls. A wide variety of wall-mounted planters are available, from simple, narrow plastic or wooden containers to self-watering polypropylene pockets that can be used en masse for a green wall effect. Green wall systems, once available only to the trade, are increasingly accessible for the home gardener—usually in the form of a DIY kit.

Choose shallow-rooted crops such as herbs, peppers, lettuce, and salad greens, and plant strawberries, trailing nasturtiums, and dwarf varieties of peas along the outside edge of containers; these spillers look pretty cascading over the side. Bear in mind that given the relatively small amount of soil these containers can hold, you will need to water frequently. Reduce the workload by installing automatic drip irrigation.

Pole beans are a natural for growing up instead of out.

MAKING THE MOST OF LIMITED SPACE

Vines in the Small Garden

Vines are perfect candidates for vertical growing. Some, such as beans or kiwi, only need to be shown a trellis and they'll start to climb; others, such as melons or cucumber, need a little more encouragement.

Annual vines include peas, pole beans, cucumbers, squash, melon, and vining (indeterminate) tomatoes; perennials include grapes and kiwi. For all, set up your vertical supports prior to planting to avoid damaging developing roots and shoots.

Annuals such as peas and beans require only moderately strong supports: plant two or three seeds at the base of each pole. Vining tomatoes can be trained upward using a variety of supports, including stakes, fences, heavy-duty cages, tomato spirals, and trellises. Whichever you choose, make sure it is at least 5 ft. tall: indeterminate tomatoes get very tall. Keeping them pruned is also key to growing vining tomatoes in a narrow space. Vining cucumbers, melons, zucchini, and gourds need a solid apparatus that can support the weight of their fruit. Lean a wooden grid or old metal gate against a wall or fence and encourage the vines to scramble over the top, supporting heavy fruits such as melon with netting. Or use an old ladder and allow developing fruit to be supported by the ladder's rungs.

Planting perennial vines such as kiwi and grapes requires planning and probably a bit of construction work. Both, but especially kiwi, need robust structures to climb and a sunny, sheltered location. Arbors and wall-mounted trellises work well.

By training them up a trellis, you can enjoy vining fruits and vegetables even in a limited area.

Stretching the Growing Season

Season-extension techniques allow you to grow food beyond the main gardening season. Start by introducing yourself to cool-season crops—if you limit yourself to tomatoes and cucumbers, your garden won't see any action until late spring or early summer. Cool-season crops such as lettuces and peas can go into the ground long before that. But you can use a few tricks to get your crops growing even earlier in the spring, or to hold the garden well into fall or winter.

Cloches

Cloches are open-bottomed protective coverings that can be placed over tender seedlings to protect them from frost and windchill. Traditional cloches were bell-shaped

A classic bell-shaped glass cloche protects a young basil seedling from frost.

(*cloche* is French for "bell"). Cloches can be made of glass, plastic, terra-cotta, or even bamboo. Cloches are great for protecting tender plants against unexpected early spring frosts or for easing seedlings out into the world during their hardening-off period. You can easily make yourself a whole supply of utilitarian cloches by cutting the bottoms off plastic jugs or bottles. Place a bottomless bottle over a seedling, gently pushing it into the soil. Just make sure to remove the cloches on hot, sunny days or you risk frying your seedlings.

Cold frames

A cold frame works on the same principle as a cloche—it protects plants by acting as a mini greenhouse—but with room for multiple plants. These simple—and potentially compact—contraptions allow you to harvest cool-season crops year-round, even in areas with cold winters. Cold frames can also give you a jump on spring by providing a sheltered place where sowed seeds can sprout and grow. (You can transplant them after the weather warms.) They can also be used as transitional housing for seedlings during their hardening-off stage.

Row covers

Floating row covers, also used to protect plants from insect pests, can make great season-extension tools. Lightweight fabrics can be laid directly over your plants or propped up with stakes or hoops. The edges can be secured with stones, handfuls of soil, or a length of wood. Like cloches and cold frames, row covers create a microclimate for the enclosed crops, raising the ambient temperature and protecting late-summer and fall crops against early frosts. Row cover fabric is available in several different weights; look for the type that offers frost protection.

Build Your Own Cold Frame

You can buy ready-made cold frames, but you can also make your own small-space version quite easily—and for almost if not entirely free—using salvaged materials.

A cold frame has two essential parts: a base, which is a frame made of plywood, reclaimed brick, old pallets, cinderblock, or even bales of hay; and a lid created from an old window, a sheet of rigid acrylic material, or thick plastic sheeting.

1 Build the base in a four-sided, rectangular shape (or whatever shape will fit your lid), positioning it where it will receive sun for most of the day. Construct the back of the base to be slightly higher than the front; this allows for maximum sun exposure and heat capture. Ideally, the walls of the base should be draft resistant to provide good insulation for tender plants.

2 The lid can be simply laid on top. You may add some weather stripping around the edges to prevent drafts. The lid can also be attached with hinges. As with cloches, the lid should be propped open or removed on hot days so that your plants don't overheat.

This small cold frame is made from salvaged wood and glass.

Plastic mulches

Spreading plastic mulches over prepared soil will allow you to plant warm-season crops such as peppers, melons, tomatoes, and cucumbers earlier in the season; the soil warms after the mulch absorbs heat from the sun. Black plastic is the most common type, which is also used for weed control and to reduce evaporation. You can also find silver, red, or green plastic mulches (each created for specific purposes or types of crops), as well as biodegradable mulches. Cover the soil a week or more before you intend to plant, burying the edges into the soil. Cut an X in the plastic wherever you want to plant, then tuck in seeds or transplants.

Winter Gardening

The ultimate in succession planting, winter gardening is all about maximizing your space and your harvest. In fact, many edibles actually taste better after a frost. They produce a natural antifreeze—sugar—that translates into a sweeter-tasting vegetable. Just one more reason to stretch your growing season.

The key to winter gardening is planting midsummer through late summer for most vegetables. Do not plant cabbage in late autumn and expect a winter harvest—it just won't happen. A winter garden is like a refrigerator: food stays fresh and ready to eat, but it doesn't put on any growth.

Some varieties of cabbage can provide winter harvests.

Day length is the critical factor. As the days get shorter, growth slows. By late fall/early winter, plants are pretty much in hibernation mode until the days start to lengthen again in early spring. The goal is to have your plants reach full size by Halloween, ready for eating throughout the winter. Don't automatically pull them out if they aren't ready, though. You can leave cold-tolerant veggies in the ground; they might surprise you by throwing out some new growth when the days start to lengthen.

It's difficult to imagine planting your winter garden in the heat of summer. One way around this is to start your winter-garden seeds in flats and transplant them into their final homes after the tomatoes and zucchini have been cleared out.

In mild climates, many veggies are happy without protection from the cold (although mulch and protection from wind and excess rain never hurts). In colder climates, cold frames may be necessary to ensure a winter harvest.

Kale is an attractive and hardy leafy green than can be harvested throughout the winter in many climates.

Mesclun greens, including mizuna, mustard, and chard, are tolerant of light frosts.

Edibles for the Winter Garden

These lists offer some suggestions for winter gardens, along
with hardiness levels. Edibles are defined as:

Hardy
(tolerates below-freezing
temperatures)

  broad beans
  broccoli, overwintering
  Brussels sprouts
  collard greens
  corn salad (mâche)
  garlic
  kale
  leeks
  parsnips
  rye
  scallions
  spinach
  turnips

Half-hardy
(withstands light frosts)

  arugula (rocket)
  beets
  bok choy
  broccoli
  celery
  endive
  fennel
  lettuce
  mesclun greens
  parsley
  peas
  radishes

Hardy or Half-hardy
(depends on selection)

  cabbage
  carrots
  cauliflower
  chard
  onions

Harvesting and Preparing for Next Year

The end of summer marks a time of plenty in the garden. If all has gone well, you are snipping fresh herbs to top every meal, snapping beans nightly, and hustling to keep up with ripening cherry tomatoes.

As the growing season winds down, it can be tempting to be done with gardening for a few months. Believe me, I know: it has been go-time since early spring, and you want a break. But before you pack it in, devote a day or two to thinking about next year's garden.

◄ Harvesting the buried treasure of potatoes that you've been growing all season is supremely satisfying.

This is also the time, if you're not planning on winter gardening, to clean and store pots and tools, and to save the seeds of the plants you want to grow again. First, however, is the fun part: the harvest. The moment you've been waiting for. Or is it? Is that pepper ready to pick, or could it use another week in the sun? Knowing when to harvest is more art than science, but some guidelines can help.

Harvesting Your Crops

Pick early and pick often. Giant zucchinis and foot-long beans may look impressive, but they will be mealy, stringy, and tasteless. And harvest frequently: thwarting your plants' attempts to produce seed encourages them to try again—and produce more.

Fruit and fruiting vegetables

You can tell when most fruits and fruiting vegetables are ready to harvest. Their color changes, often from green to red. Usually, they get softer; they may also become fragrant. Many tree fruits are ready to harvest if, when given a gentle twist, they drop into your palm. (Pears are a notable exception and should be picked when unripe.)

Herbs

Leafy herbs should be harvested frequently throughout the growing season by pinching back the most vigorous growth, which encourages them to become bushier and more prolific. Pick herbs just before eating for the most intense flavor. Large quantities can be dried or frozen at the end of the season. Chop fresh herbs, place them in ice cube trays, top with water, and freeze for later use. Or cut perennial herb stems just above soil level and hang them to dry in a cool, dry place.

Leafy and root vegetables

Harvest the outer leaves of leafy greens such as chard, lettuce, and kale as soon as plants are large enough to spare a few, or treat them as a cut-and-come again crop and cut them back to an inch above the ground. More leaves will usually appear for a second and third harvest. Like most vegetables, lettuce and salad greens are best when harvested young; overly mature lettuce is bitter and tough.

It can be difficult to judge when root crops are ready for harvesting. Beets and carrots often start to poke out of the ground when they are ripe. Garlic, bulb onions, and potatoes indicate readiness through their dying leaves and stems.

A striped eggplant grown on a balcony is ready for picking.

Saving Seeds

Saving seeds has recently gone from simply being a thrifty mode of plant propagation to a bold political statement. Although the original motivations are still valid—to save money and sow plants that perform well under local conditions—more than ever, people are saving seeds for other reasons.

Hybrids and heirlooms

The majority of commercially sold seeds are hybrids, often a deliberate cross between two different parent plants. Hybrids are selected for traits desired by the breeder. That might be flavor, but in industrial agriculture, hybrids are judged by their ability to store well or withstand long-distance shipping. Hybrid seeds, which are identified F1 (first filial generation) on the packet, are genetically identical. As a result, the seeds of hybrid plants may be sterile or may revert to characteristics of one of the parent plants. Because one can never be certain what they will produce, hybrid seeds aren't usually saved by gardeners.

Open-pollinated (OP) plants are the other side of the coin. These plants are pollinated by wind, bees, and other pollinators and, in many cases, produce viable seed that will produce a plant just like its parent. In fact, plants grown from OP seeds you have saved may even perform better than the original plants the year before,

Parsley benefits from being harvested regularly.

Pea seeds are some of the easiest to save. Let the pods dry on the vines before removing the seeds.

because they have started to adjust to the conditions of your microclimate. Although F1 seeds are static, OP seeds adapt. This preservation of a diverse plant gene pool is one of the major reasons for growing open-pollinated edibles (being able to save your own seeds is the other).

Heirloom vegetables and fruits are always open pollinated. Although no one can quite agree on how old a particular selection needs to be to be considered an heirloom, most of these plants were in existence prior to World War II and the advent of industrial agriculture. Some are centuries old. Heirloom edibles are not grown in the large-scale commercial monocultures that supply most supermarket produce, but they are often incredibly flavorful and weirdly beautiful. Growing and saving heirloom seed helps to keep these older types of edibles alive and pushes back against the increasing homogenization of our food supply.

So—should you avoid hybrid seed? My view is an unequivocal "mostly." Hybrid plants can be quite useful, such as those bred for disease-resistance, to ripen early, or to take up less space. These are all good things. But if hybrids were all we grew, we would be participating in the extinction of older open-pollinated selections. So my aim is to grow mostly OP seed. Besides, growing produce that cannot be found in grocery stores is half the fun. Seek out rare and unusual plants through seed-saving organizations or reputable seed companies that trade in organic, non-GMO seeds. And, whenever possible, save your own.

Collecting and storing seeds

Saving the seeds of some vegetables, such as peas and peppers, is straightforward: collect, clean, dry, and store. Others, such as corn and cucumber, are a little more complicated, requiring separation from other plants to prevent random cross-pollination (producing seed that does not accurately reproduce the parent plant). Another class of vegetables, which includes carrots and cabbages, not only requires separation, but needs more than a year to produce seed.

When you are starting out in seed saving, try seeds of open-pollinated beans, dill, cilantro, lettuce, peas, peppers, and tomatoes. These edibles offer your best chance for success, especially if you grow only one type of each crop.

If you feel lucky, try saving the seeds of OP corn, cucumber, melon, radish, and squash, providing you are growing only one type. (Commercial growers separate these plants by at least half a mile; less for corn.)

Whichever seeds you save, your first item of business is to identify the plants that produced solidly or the earliest, or that resisted disease the best. In essence, seed saving makes you a backyard plant breeder, allowing you to continue the lineage of strong performers—so choose wisely.

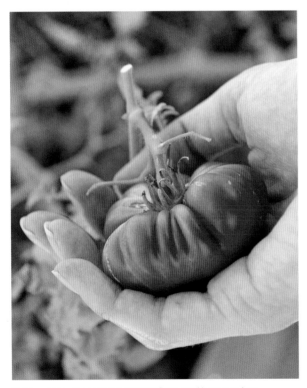

Heirloom tomatoes are fun to grow from seed because they often look nothing like the average supermarket variety.

Saving seeds from nonfruiting herbs and vegetables.
Bolting occurs when cool-season crops such as radishes and lettuce decide it's high time to make some babies. In spring or early summer, we want to prevent bolting, but for end-of-season seed-saving purposes, we want plants to bolt. They send up a stalk, which grows tall and eventually flowers. We collect the seeds from the flowers or pods produced.

Saving these types of seeds is easiest if you allow them to ripen and dry on the plant. Then you can clip them off, brush off any bugs or dirt, and tuck the heads into paper bags until they are completely dry. Sometimes it's better to cut off the seedpods or flower heads before they are fully ripe. Strong winds and wet weather can scatter seeds and cause rot, so if nasty weather is imminent, cut off the seed heads and hang them upside down in a dry, well-ventilated spot. Tie a paper bag around each seed head to collect the seeds as they drop. Once the seed heads are completely dry, tease the seeds from their pods.

Saving seeds from fruiting vegetables. The seeds from fruiting vegetables are harvested wet. The fruits should be picked when fully ripe, cut open, and the seeds removed. Spoon the seeds (and inevitable pulp) into a mesh colander or sieve for washing. Try to remove all the pulp. Some seeds, such as those of peppers and melons, are easily cleaned; just set them aside on a plate or towel to dry before storing.

Select seeds from the best plants with the most desirable characteristics.

Dill seeds drop easily when they are dry; cut off the seed heads and carefully store them in a paper bag until they are completely dry. Then tuck them away for next year.

Saving Tomato Seeds

Tomato seeds require special treatment; they are protected by a growth-inhibiting gel coating that must be removed before you store them. But if you have a particularly prolific plant, or one that produces delicious tomatoes, it's worth the effort.

MATERIALS

1 tomato from an especially high-quality OP plant
Mason jar
Approximately one cup of water
Cheesecloth or towel
Plate or towel for drying

1 Cut the tomato in half.

2 Scoop out and rinse the seeds.

3 Place seeds in a mason jar with the water.

4 Cover the opening with cheesecloth or a towel.

5 Place the jar in a warm, out-of-the-way location (the mixture is going to reek).

6 Start checking for signs of fermentation after a couple days. When you see a layer of mold growing on the surface, the seeds are ready.

7 Scoop off the top layer of mold, immature seeds, and other gunk; viable seeds will have settled on the bottom.

8 Rinse the viable seeds under running water, and transfer them to a plate to dry.

Saving tomato seeds takes some effort, but you'll be glad you did next harvest season.

Storing seeds. Seal seeds in labeled paper envelopes or small, airtight jars (paper envelopes should be enclosed in an airtight container), then stash them in the refrigerator or another cool, dry place. Heat and humidity spell certain death for most seeds. Stored properly, many seeds will last for up to three or more years. (Onions, garlic, chives, leeks, and parsnips are an exception; sow these seeds within a year.)

Making New Plants by Taking Cuttings

Not all edibles are best propagated by seed. Many herbs and shrubs are often propagated by cuttings, and fruit tree scions (twig cuttings) are grafted onto desirable rootstocks. Although grafting is an art best left to experts and enthusiastic hobbyists, taking cuttings requires no more than a sharp knife and a little know-how.

Soft-stemmed herbs such as mint and basil readily grow roots when placed in water. Take a cutting by snipping off the top 3 to 6 in. from a lower side shoot, just below a pair of leaves. Remove the bottom leaves and place the cutting in a glass of water. Change the water every couple of days. Roots should appear within two weeks. The cutting can then be gently transplanted into potting soil.

In the same way, you can take cuttings of the new spring growth of woody-stemmed herbs, such as rosemary and sage, and shrubs such as blueberry. Instead of rooting them in water, however, place the cuttings in potting soil. You may want to dip the cuttings in rooting hormone to help encourage root formation. Keep the pots well watered, out of direct sun, and enclosed in a plastic bag to hold humidity (the bag should not touch the plant's leaves). The cuttings will root in four to six weeks.

Winding Down in the Garden

Even if you plan to winter garden, at some point in late summer or autumn, depending on your locale, it will be time to prepare for the off-season. The main objectives of the big fall cleanup are to protect your soil from erosion caused by winter rains and to remove opportunities for pests and diseases to proliferate.

Remove plant debris. After the last of your vegetables have been harvested, pull out the plants, plus any weeds and fallen leaves, and add them to the compost pile if you have one. To avoid cursing yourself with a new generation of problems, do not compost diseased or pest-ridden plants, perennial weeds, or weed seeds. Those should go in the trash. Leave hardy or half-hardy plants in the ground and continue to harvest edibles as long as you can.

Basil roots easily in water.

Cover the soil. If you have been nurturing along some transplants for a fall and winter harvest, plant these as soon as possible. If you didn't get around to starting or buying transplants, sow a cover crop (green mulch) or spread on a layer of compost or leaf mulch to reduce erosion and improve the soil.

Protect tender plants. Unless you are lucky enough to live where the ground never freezes, you need to protect nonhardy or marginally hardy perennials from the ravages of winter. This is especially true of container plantings, which are less insulated from the cold than inground plants.

No matter how small your garden, there is usually debris to clean up come autumn.

Tender plants should be lifted and brought indoors for the winter. Potted herbs such as rosemary will make do on a bright windowsill; larger plants can ride out the winter in an unheated garage, as long as the temperature inside stays above freezing. Borderline hardy plants can be protected with a thick layer of mulch, or they can be wrapped with burlap or heavyweight row-cover fabric.

Clean and store tools. Collect empty containers and remove any remaining dirt or plant debris. Scrub them out with soapy water, or leave them to soak overnight in a 9:1 solution of water and hydrogen peroxide.

Collect stakes and tomato cages and store them out of the rain or snow. Gardening tools can also be cleaned at this time. At the least, wipe them down with soapy water, and then dry them thoroughly before storing. Pruning shears should be sterilized with a quick dip in a 1:2 hydrogen peroxide and water bath to prevent the spread of disease. The heads of shovels, hoes, and other tools with metal parts can be cleaned and oiled in one go: mix some oil into a bucket of coarse sand and poke in your shovels and pruning shears. Wipe off the sand and your tools are ready for winter hibernation. And so are you.

Reflect. Once the garden has been put to bed, you can relax and look back on your successes. If this was your first garden, you deserve congratulations! If your experience was like mine, it was interesting, motivating, and, above all, satisfying. If your garden (or its produce) failed to live up to your expectations, take this time to reassess.

What crops tasted the best? Which crops were the easiest to grow? How can you replicate your successes?

Which crops were planted too late, didn't get enough sun, or were plagued by pests? What are you going to do about it next time?

What vegetables did you grow but not eat—because, it turns out, you don't really like eggplant, or cabbage, or kale? Should you have planted more of another vegetable?

What did you see in other gardeners' gardens, seed catalogues, books, or magazines, that you want to try next year?

I believe that, no matter how much you read, research, or plan, gardening is a lifelong learning process—a (mostly) joyful experiment in trial and error. Like me, you will make plenty of errors, and that's okay. Some years will be incredible—you'll harvest tons of perfectly delicious, blemish-free produce and smugly admit that you're a natural at this gardening thing. Other years your garden will limp along, crippled by poor weather, pests, and your two-week vacation, during which your neighbor failed to water as promised. Shake it off. Know that next year will be different. Growing your own food—no matter how small the space—is not a destination, but a journey to be enjoyed every step of the way.

Wrapping the base and containers of potted fruit trees helps protect them from winter temperatures.

Edibles from A to Z

From apples to zucchini, details on when, how, and what to plant in your small space are included here. Use this part of the book as a quick reference resource when you need info, pronto. You can also use this information as a planning tool and a source of inspiration while you are developing a planting scheme for the new season.

Not all of the edibles mentioned are suited to growing in containers or in tiny spaces. They are included, however, because some gardeners might choose to devote all their available space to growing one fantastic, stately artichoke plant. Others might have a bit more room and decide to give a full-sized fruit tree a try.

Each listing includes recommendations for a number of great cultivars, and I've highlighted those that are especially well suited to small spaces. I believe, however, that you can find the best edibles to grow by talking to other gardeners in your area. A tomato that performs amazingly in one area might be a flop in another, so ask at a favorite nursery or talk to neighbors for their recommendations.

Finally, a note about hardiness: for perennial plants, hardiness zones indicate the temperature range in which a particular plant will thrive. If you don't know what your zone is, search "plant hardiness zone" online. However, not all cultivars within a species will necessarily be hardy to the zone indicated; great variation can exist in the hardiness of different cultivars. In addition, container-grown plants will be less hardy than those grown in the ground—keep that in mind when you are choosing what to grow and where to grow it.

◀ Sun-loving herbs get plenty of light on this terrace, while an espaliered fruit tree in the background has a trellis for support.

APPLE

Malus domestica
Deciduous tree, hardy in zones 3–9

If you thought you couldn't have an orchard on a balcony, think again. With dwarfing rootstocks that make it possible to grow trees as small as 4 ft. tall and 2 ft. wide, pruning and training techniques that create espaliered trees that grow low and flat against a fence or wall, and grafting methods that produce three or more types of apple on one tree, the apple is the ultimate small-space fruit tree. The only catch is that most apples will not self-pollinate, meaning you must plant at least two trees of different types (or one grafted tree with multiple apple selections) or you won't get any fruit.

START Apples do not reproduce accurately from seed; instead, they are grown by grafting a scion (the trunk and upper part of the tree, or a branch of a tree) onto a root-stock, which determines the tree's final size and hardiness. Trees can be transplanted from fall through spring. Spring is better for those in cold climates; warm-climate gardeners can plant in the fall. Formative pruning should also be done in the late fall or winter. Many apples, especially those grown on dwarfing rootstocks, should be staked.

GROW Place trees in full sun, in moist, well-drained soil. Apples do not actually require pruning, but it can help produce a desirable shape and improve fruit production. Spray with a horticultural oil in late winter to kill overwintering pests if they were problems in the past. In spring, mulch with compost, avoiding the trunk and root crown area, and scratch a complete organic fertilizer into the soil. This is also the time to hang codling moth traps and apply sticky tree bands if codling moths are a problem in your area. Thinning—removing fruit while it is still developing—allows the remaining fruit to grow larger, improves next year's production, and reduces the chance that limbs will break under the weight of a heavy crop. Thin apples when they are 1 in. in diameter, leaving only one apple per cluster. Thinning is especially crucial in new trees; strip all blossoms and fruit from trees during their first year.

HARVEST Dwarf apples take a couple of years or more to produce a good harvest; standard types may not produce fruit until their fifth year. Trees are usually at least a year old when you purchase them at the nursery. Apples are ready to harvest in late summer or early fall, depending on the type. Ripe apples will come away from the tree with a gentle twist.

ADVICE Choose an apple tree based on your climate, your available space, and your eating preferences. Multiple-grafted trees are great small-space options because they are self-fertile—more than one type of apple is grafted onto one rootstock, so you need only one tree—and you get to try a few different types of apples. Alternatively, plant two or more columnar selections—dwarf trees with very short branches and a bottlebrush appearance. They measure only 2 ft. wide and are often less than 6 ft. tall.

IN CONTAINERS Dwarf and columnar apples do well in containers; choose a large container or half-barrel at least 2 ft. deep.

PROBLEMS Aphids, codling moth, fire blight, plum curculio, powdery mildew, scab.

POPULAR SELECTIONS In small spaces, choose trees on dwarfing rootstocks such as M27, M26, Mark, or M9. Talk to a reputable nursery or orchardist for recommendations for your area. If you can have only one tree, make sure it is a self-pollinating cultivar such as 'Granny Smith' or 'Golden Delicious' (though even these trees will produce better if cross-pollinated with another type of apple) or choose an espaliered tree grafted with two or more varieties. In areas with mild winters, choose cultivars that do not require long, cold winters to set fruit, such as 'Dorsett Golden' or 'Anna'. Other popular apples include 'Bramley's Seedling', 'Northern Spy', and 'Liberty' for pies and cooking; and 'Cox's Orange Pippin', 'Fiesta', 'Honeycrisp', and 'Gala' for fresh eating.

SUITED TO SMALL SPACES

'Scarlet Sentinel', 'Golden Sentinel', and 'Northpole' are popular columnar cultivars.

APRICOT

Prunus armeniaca
Deciduous tree, hardy in zones 5–9

With their showy pink or white blossoms, apricots make beautiful specimen trees for the small garden. Late spring frosts are the major hindrance to apricot growing; frost kills the blossoms, reducing fruit yield. If late frosts are an issue in your area, look for apricots that bloom later in the spring. Unlike apples, most apricots are self-pollinating,

'Queen Cox' apple is a self-pollinating form of the popular 'Cox's Orange Pippen'.

Apricot, *continued*

although a tree will produce more fruit if grown close to another type of apricot. Dwarf trees can be grown in containers.

START Bare-root or container-grown trees can be transplanted from fall through spring. Spring is better for those in cold climates; gardeners in warmer climates can plant them in the fall.

GROW In full sun and a sheltered location, in moist, well-drained soil. Train into an open-vase shape or espalier into a fan shape, pruning after the tree has flowered. Thinning—removing fruit while it is still developing—allows the remaining fruit to grow larger, improves next year's production, and reduces the chance that limbs will break under the weight of a heavy crop. Thin apricots when they are small, leaving 2 to 3 in. between fruits—even more when the tree is young.

HARVEST In midsummer to late summer, once the fruit is even in color and slightly soft.

ADVICE Even if you choose a late-blooming apricot, unexpected frosts can cause damage. Protect blossoms from impending frosts by covering the tree with a light sheet or cloth.

IN CONTAINERS Choose a dwarf tree and a large container or half-barrel at least 20 in. deep.

PROBLEMS Bacterial canker, brown rot, leafhoppers, mites, nematodes, powdery mildew, verticillium wilt.

POPULAR SELECTIONS Many apricots are available in both standard and dwarfing rootstocks; be sure to choose a dwarfing rootstock such as 'Pixie'. Also choose self-fertile types that bloom after your area's average last frost date. 'Harglow' and 'Tilton' are self-pollinating and late-blooming varieties; 'Royal Blenheim' is the classic semi-dwarf California apricot—good for areas with mild winters.

ARTICHOKE

Cynara scolymus
Tender perennial, grown as an annual in areas with cold winters, hardy to zone 7

These large, tender perennials produce gorgeous thistle-like flower buds that are coveted for their delicious hearts. Artichokes make beautiful focal points in any garden; however, their large size makes them less than suitable for very small spaces.

START Start indoors eight to twelve weeks before the last frost; transplant outside after the last frost. Space plants 3 ft. apart.

GROW In a sheltered, full-sun location with well-drained, fertile soil. Artichokes are heavy feeders; amend the soil with compost prior to planting and fertilize with a potassium-rich fertilizer throughout the growing season.

HARVEST In summer, cut flower buds 2 to 3 in. below the base just before they begin to open.

ADVICE In areas with mild winters, protect plants with a thick layer of mulch and try growing as perennials; artichokes produce best in their second year.

IN CONTAINERS Since artichokes can grow 3 to 5 ft. tall and wide, they are not great candidates for container growing. If you are determined, however, grow one plant per half-barrel–sized container and fertilize regularly.

PROBLEMS Slugs.

POPULAR SELECTIONS 'Green Globe' and 'Imperial Star' will produce buds in their first year.

ARUGULA

see Lettuce and salad greens

Artichokes often produce one large flower, with smaller buds emerging beneath it.

ASIAN GREENS

Brassica juncea and *B. rapa*
Hardy and half-hardy, cool-season annuals

Asian greens is a catchall term for leafy greens in the brassica family. They are often grown as a cut-and-come-again crop, harvested young and eaten raw in salads, or, when larger, tossed in a stir-fry. They include a variety of leafy mustards, mizuna, komatsuna, and mibuna, and sometimes bok choy (a type of Chinese cabbage). You can often find a blend of these seeds packaged together and sold as Asian Greens or Spicy Mix.

START Direct sow in early spring, succession sowing every few weeks until the summer heat hits. Sow again in late summer for a fall harvest. Scatter seeds evenly across moist soil and cover them with a thin layer of soil—or scratch seeds into the surface.

GROW In full sun, in fertile, moist, well-drained soil. Asian greens enjoy full sun when the weather is cool, but some shade is helpful in preventing bolting during warm weather. Add lime to acidic soils prior to planting and amend with manure, compost, or a complete organic fertilizer.

HARVEST When plants are 4 to 6 in. tall, cut back to 1 or 2 in. above the soil surface. Leaves will resprout, providing several more harvests. Harvest greens frequently for the best flavor.

ADVICE Asian greens are attractive additions to the cool-season garden and for edging containers or beds. Some are hardy and will overwinter in all but the coldest climates.

PROBLEMS Aphids, flea beetles.

IN CONTAINERS Good even in small (6 in. deep) containers.

POPULAR SELECTIONS 'Red Giant' mustard has large, burgundy leaves—it tastes mild when harvested in cool weather and tangy when harvested in the heat.

SUITED TO SMALL SPACES
Prolific and mild, mizuna can be grown all winter long in mild-winter areas.

ASPARAGUS

Asparagus officinalis
Cool-season perennial, hardy in zones 2–9

An asparagus bed is a long-term commitment. This long-lived perennial needs a lot of space—growing up to 5 ft. tall and just as wide—as well as time to mature. But once started, it produces one of the earliest and most delicious spring vegetables.

START Purchase year-old crowns (roots). Transplant them outside after the last frost.

GROW In full sun or part shade. Plant crowns in a deep (12 in.) trench or hole amended with manure or compost, spacing plants 18 in. apart. Gradually add more soil as shoots emerge, without covering the tips. Mulch with compost or manure every spring, prior to the emergence of shoots.

HARVEST Do not harvest spears until the third spring, allowing the resulting leafy fronds to nourish the roots. In the third year, harvest spears by snapping or cutting them off at ground level when they are 5 to 10 in. tall. Stop harvesting when the emerging spears start to grow thinner; allow them to grow into tall, ferny foliage that will support next year's harvest. Remove the foliage in fall to prevent asparagus beetles from overwintering.

ADVICE White asparagus, expensive to buy in stores, is simply regular asparagus that has been kept out of the sun. Grow your own by covering the growing spears with mulch or plastic pots.

IN CONTAINERS Not recommended.

PROBLEMS Asparagus beetles, fusarium wilt, rust.

POPULAR SELECTIONS Choose male hybrids (which produce the best spears) such as 'Jersey Knight', 'Jersey Giant', or UC 157.

BASIL

Ocimum spp.
Tender annual

A mainstay of Italian and Asian cooking, basil is a beautiful and hard-working addition to any edible garden. When grown with tomatoes, it is said to improve their flavor. Basil also repels aphids and mites.

START Start seeds indoors four to six weeks prior to the last frost, or direct sow seeds once the soil has warmed. Space plants 12 in. apart.

GROW In full to part sun, in a warm, sheltered location. Soil should be rich, consistently moist, and well drained. Pinch out the growing tips beginning when the plant is about 4 in. tall to encourage bushy growth and inhibit flowering.

HARVEST Harvest regularly, pinching off the tips of the stems. Best eaten fresh, basil can also be frozen, dried, or preserved in oil.

ADVICE If you have a bright, sunny windowsill available, move your pot of basil indoors at the end of summer to prolong the harvest.

IN CONTAINERS Excellent in containers at least 4 in. deep.

PROBLEMS Slugs, verticillium wilt.

POPULAR SELECTIONS Italian selections include the classics for pesto: 'Sweet Basil', 'Purple Ruffles', and 'Cinnamon', which are also beautifully ornamental. 'Pesto Perpetuo' is an unusual, variegated, creamy white and green variety that rarely goes to seed. Thai, lemon, and holy basil are more often used in Asian cooking.

SUITED TO SMALL SPACES

'Genovese' is especially good for pesto. 'Siam Queen' has a variety of uses in Thai, Vietnamese, and other southeast Asian cuisines.

Pinching sweet basil flower buds produces leaves; allowing flowers attracts beneficial bugs.

BEAN

Phaseolus spp. and *Glycine max*
Warm-season annual

Beans should be on everyone's must-grow list: no super-market bean can compare to the taste of homegrown, fresh-picked beans. They are one of the easiest vegetables to start from seed and are equally easy to grow. In fact, the toughest part is often choosing which type to plant.

Beans are a diverse group. Some are climbers; others are short and bushy. But the biggest distinction among them is the stage at which they are harvested. Snap beans, also known as green, wax, or string beans, are harvested young and eaten whole, including the pod. Shelling beans, also called horticultural beans, are harvested and shelled when the beans have swelled in the pods but are still tender. (Note that fava beans, which are broad beans, are not included in this discussion and are covered in the section on broad beans.)

START Direct sow after the soil has really warmed up—usually in late spring. Seeds will rot in cool, wet soil. Plant seeds 4 to 8 in. apart in moistened soil, and avoid watering until they have sprouted. In areas with wet, cool springs, start beans indoors and plant them out after the weather has stabilized—but be extremely gentle when transplanting because they don't like to be moved. Using a legume inoculant on seeds or in the planting hole prior to planting encourages healthy growth by introducing beneficial microorganisms that increase the availability of nitrogen in your soil. You can find inoculants online or at garden centers.

GROW In full sun, in well-drained soil. Bush beans do not require support, but climbers need a teepee or another vertical support. Set up supports prior to planting to avoid inadvertently damaging the growing roots.

HARVEST Harvest frequently (daily is best) to encourage greater production, preferably when the plant's leaves are dry to avoid spreading disease. Pick snap and other beans eaten in the pod when they are small and still tender; after the seeds start to swell, the pods become stringy. Shelling beans, lima beans, and soybeans can be harvested after the seeds have swelled but are still green and tender.

ADVICE In small spaces, pole and runner beans make excellent use of vertical space. You can also train these climbers over trellises to provide shade to heat-sensitive crops. Many beans have pretty flowers or interesting pods in colors ranging from purple to yellow (wax) or even striped.

IN CONTAINERS Bush and dwarf types do well in containers that are at least 9 in. deep; climbers prefer large tubs or half-barrels.

PROBLEMS Aphids, bacterial blight, leafhoppers, Mexican bean beetle, rust, slugs.

POPULAR SELECTIONS Lima beans (*Phaseolus lunatus*): 'Henderson Bush' is compact; 'Christmas' is a pretty climber. Runner beans (*P. coccineus*): 'Scarlet Runner' is an attractive heirloom runner bean cultivar; 'White Emergo' is a white-flowering cultivar. Snap beans (*P. vulgaris*): 'Kentucky Wonder' and 'Romano' are classics, available as bush or pole growers. 'Golden Child' is a wax (yellow) bean well suited for containers; 'Royal Burgundy' produces purple pods on a bush plant. Soybeans (*Glycine max*): 'Early Hakucho' produces early; 'Sayamusume' has great flavor.

SUITED TO SMALL SPACES
'Blue Lake' is a classic snap bean; 'Fortex' is a French filet pole bean that produces tender, slender pods.

BEET

Beta vulgaris
Half-hardy, cool-season biennials grown
as annuals

With their attractive and edible leaves, delicious roots, and ability to produce in less than full sun, beets make an excellent crop for beginners. Also known as beetroot, beets are available in a variety of root shapes and colors beyond basic beet red.

START Direct sow at the time of last frost, succession sowing every two to three weeks until midsummer. Space 1 to 2 in. apart, thinning to 5 in. apart when plants are 2 in. tall.

GROW In fertile, well-drained, consistently moist soil with added compost. Beets grow well in full sun or part shade.

HARVEST Start by harvesting and eating the thinned seedlings, and then progress to snipping off the occasional outer leaf as the plants develop. Roots can be harvested in six to fourteen weeks, depending on the type. They are best harvested young; older beets become woody.

ADVICE Keep beets well watered; dry soil causes roots to become woody or split. They may bolt in hot weather, so harvest them before the heat hits or provide some shade.

IN CONTAINERS The smaller, rounded selections are best for container growing. Choose containers with a depth of at least 10 in.

PROBLEMS Flea beetles, leaf miners, slugs.

POPULAR SELECTIONS 'Touchstone Gold' has orange roots and gold-veined leaves; hybrid 'Red Ace'

starts out quickly in spring and can be harvested year-round in areas with mild winters. I like to plant a variety of colors for an attractive plate.

SUITED TO SMALL SPACES
'Chioggia' is an heirloom cultivar that produces red-and-white–striped roots.

Beet greens are delicious and nutritious, but overharvesting will reduce root size.

BLACKBERRY AND BLACKBERRY HYBRIDS

Rubus spp.
Perennial cane fruit, hardy in zones 5–9

Blackberries are one of the quintessential summer fruits. Although you can often find them growing wild, cultivating them at home allows you to select a thornless type or choose one of the many hybrids available. Blackberry canes are either trailing and thicket-forming or erect and somewhat self-supporting. The blackberry hybrids, which include boysenberry, loganberry, tayberry, youngberry, and dewberry, are usually in the trailing class. Their canes are long and vinelike and should be tied to a support. The erect types are shorter and do not require trellising; these are also more cold tolerant. Don't expect berries your first summer: blackberries produce fruit on second-year canes.

START Purchase bare-root or container-grown plants. Transplant them from fall through spring. Spring is better for those in cold climates; gardeners in warm climates can plant in the fall.

GROW In full or part sun in a sheltered location. Soil should be rich in organic matter, moist, and well drained.

Space erect types 2 ft. apart; trailing types require 5 ft. or more between plants. Plant against a trellis, fence, or wire support, and tie up new fruit-bearing canes as they appear, starting in the second year. After harvest, cut back the canes that produced fruit that summer to the ground, leaving the newer canes to produce fruit for next year. For protection against extreme winter temperatures, bend the canes to the ground and mulch with straw for the winter.

HARVEST Early to late summer, depending on the selection.

ADVICE If kept in check, these vertical growers do not take up too much space. Train them up the side of the garage, in the back alley, or along any fence.

IN CONTAINERS You can grow blackberries in large (half-barrel–sized) containers, but these vigorous plants are more suited to inground gardening.

PROBLEMS Birds, powdery mildew, verticillium wilt.

POPULAR SELECTIONS 'Chester' is a semi-erect, thornless cultivar that is extremely cold tolerant; 'Triple Crown' is a trailing, thornless berry that is also hardy; 'Ouachita' is an erect, thornless plant that ripens early and is suited to warmer climates. Also try hybrids such as the loganberry, a cross between blackberry and raspberry, and boysenberry, a cross between blackberry, loganberry, and raspberry.

BLUEBERRY AND CRANBERRY

Vaccinium spp.
Deciduous perennial shrubs, hardy
in zones 3–9

With their pretty spring flowers, attractive summer berries, and brilliant fall color, blueberries and cranberries make excellent shrubs for the edible landscape or ornamental border. Huckleberries and lingonberries are also members of this genus. For all, the major growing requirement is acidic soil—pH 5.0 or lower. Plant more than one type to ensure cross-pollination and good fruit production.

START Purchase bare-root or container-grown plants, or take a cutting from a friend's plant. Transplant from fall through spring. Spring is better for those in cold climates; warm-climate gardeners can plant in the fall. Space plants 4 ft. apart.

GROW In full or part sun, in well-drained, moist, acidic soil. Amend soil with pine shavings, pine needles, peat, coffee grounds, or sulfur prior to planting. If your soil naturally tends toward neutral (pH 7.0) or alkaline (above pH 7.0), grow these shrubs in large containers and provide suitable soil. Water regularly, and mulch in the spring, starting in the second year. During the first year, strip off any flower buds to force the plant to put energy into root development. Starting in the third year, practice regular annual pruning.

HARVEST Starting the second year, harvest berries in early summer through fall, depending on the plant.

Blueberries will be deep blue and sweet; cranberries ripen to bright red.

ADVICE Lowbush blueberries are the smallest, at under 2 ft. tall. Rabbiteye blueberry shrubs can reach 10 ft. or taller. Lowbush blueberries are extremely cold hardy but do not do well in warm-winter areas, because they require a cold, dormant period. Highbush blueberries are the most flexible, thriving in a range of climates.

IN CONTAINERS Good in containers at least 20 in. deep as long as the soil is acidic.

PROBLEMS Birds, botrytis blight, powdery mildew.

POPULAR SELECTIONS Blueberries: Extremely hardy 'Northsky' lowbush blueberry is well suited to container growing; 'Blueray' and 'Bluecrop' are hardy and vigorous highbush types; 'Powder Blue' is a late-ripening rabbiteye cultivar suited to areas with warm winters. 'Pink

Low-maintenance blueberries are an ideal small-space berry shrub.

Blueberries, *continued*

Lemonade' produces pink berries. Cranberries: 'Ben Lear' is an early-ripening cultivar; 'Stevens' is a widely grown commercial hybrid. Others: Try evergreen or deciduous huckleberries (*Vaccinium ovatum* and *V. parvifolium*) and lingonberries (*V. vitis-idaea*).

SUITED TO SMALL SPACES

Self-pollinating 'Top Hat' works well in containers.

BOK CHOY

see Chinese cabbage

BROAD BEAN

Vicia faba
Hardy, cool-season annual

Broad beans, also known as fava or horse beans, are unusual because they are cool-season beans. Whereas snap and shelling beans are decidedly heat-seeking, broad beans are hardy in all but the coldest climates. These large plants are useful as an overwintering crop. Some people, particularly those with Mediterranean ancestry, are strongly allergic to broad beans.

START Direct sow in late fall or early spring. Space 10 in. apart.

GROW In full sun, in well-drained soil. Pinch back tips to encourage bushiness.

HARVEST When pods are plump and tender for shelling. The leaves are also edible.

ADVICE Broad beans are often used as a trap crop because they are irresistible to aphids.

IN CONTAINERS It is possible to grow broad beans in large containers; however, their size makes them more suited to inground gardening.

PROBLEMS Aphids, bacterial blight, leafhoppers, Mexican bean beetle, rust, slugs.

POPULAR SELECTIONS 'Broad Windsor' is a classic; 'Optica' is compact.

BROCCOLI

Brassica oleracea var. *botrytis*
Half-hardy, cool-season annual

Broccoli is a cool-season annual that produces clusters of edible flowers. Some form a single head, but others produce smaller heads on multiple side shoots.

START Start seeds indoors four to six weeks before the last frost date, or direct sow in the garden at that time. Space 12 in. apart. Plant again in midsummer for a fall or winter harvest.

GROW Broccoli can be challenging for the beginner. It requires full sun, consistent moisture, and rich, fertile soil. Amend the soil with manure, compost, or a complete organic fertilizer before planting. In acidic soils, broccoli will benefit from the addition of lime.

HARVEST Cut stems with a sharp knife before the flower heads open. Once the main head is cut, secondary stems will develop; keep picking broccoli heads to encourage production.

ADVICE Try hardy sprouting broccoli, which produces small heads on long shoots, for your winter garden. To reduce problems from pests and disease, do not grow broccoli in the same place in consecutive years.

IN CONTAINERS Choose a compact type suited to container growing and a container at least 10 in. deep.

PROBLEMS Aphids, cabbage maggot, caterpillars, club-root, cutworms, leaf miners, mildew.

POPULAR SELECTIONS 'Natalino' is a compact Romanesco cultivar.

SUITED TO SMALL SPACES

Choose 'Everest' for container gardens and purple-sprouting broccoli for a multitude of colorful heads.

BRUSSELS SPROUTS

Brassica oleracea var. *gemmifera*
Half-hardy, cool-season annual

These cool-season curiosities are not well suited for very small spaces, but they are wonderful eaten fresh from the garden after a touch of frost.

START Start seeds indoors six weeks prior to the last frost for your area, or in midsummer for the winter garden. Set transplants 20 in. apart.

Broccoli thrives in cool weather; provide a thick layer of mulch in hot temperatures.

Brussels sprouts, *continued*

GROW In full sun, in fertile, well-drained soil. Keep plants evenly moist and well mulched. Brussels sprouts do best in cooler temperatures.

HARVEST Slice or snap off well-formed sprouts before they begin to open, starting at the bottom of the stalk. Upper sprouts will continue to mature. If possible, harvest after a frost for sweeter sprouts.

ADVICE To force the sprouts to mature at once, pinch out the top of the stalk after the lowest sprouts have reached ½ to 1 in. in size; you'll get a full stalk of mature sprouts in a couple of weeks.

IN CONTAINERS Suited to large containers or half-barrels.

PROBLEMS Aphids, cabbage maggot, caterpillars, clubroot, cutworms, mildew.

POPULAR SELECTIONS 'Oliver' is vigorous and compact; 'Red Bull' has attractive red foliage and sprouts.

CABBAGE

Brassica oleracea var. *capitata*
Half-hardy, cool-season biennial grown as an annual

It might seem silly to grow such a cheaply available crop at home, but cabbage can be quite a striking addition to a veggie patch or ornamental bed. Several types of cabbages can be grown year-round in most climates.

START For summer harvests, start indoors four weeks prior to the last frost. For fall and winter harvests, start indoors or outdoors in midsummer. Start overwintering cabbages indoors in midsummer, transplanting out in late summer; harvest the following spring. Space plants 24 to 36 in. apart.

GROW In full sun, in well-drained, consistently moist, fertile soil amended with abundant organic matter. Cabbage prefers cooler temperatures and can benefit from shade during hot weather. Add lime to acidic soils prior to planting. A dose of complete organic fertilizer can be beneficial, because cabbage is a heavy feeder.

HARVEST Cut off well-formed heads at the base; smaller heads will often develop for a second crop.

ADVICE Most cabbage is slow to mature and takes up a lot of space in the garden. Use it as an anchor plant in an ornamental display, or plant overwintering selections to make good use of space when not much else is in the ground.

IN CONTAINERS Choose dwarf cabbage types and containers at least 10 in. deep.

PROBLEMS Aphids, cabbage maggot, caterpillars, clubroot, cutworms, mildew.

POPULAR SELECTIONS Smooth-leaved green cabbages: 'Early Jersey Wakefield' is an heirloom for summer harvest. Crinkle-leaved (savoy) green cabbages: plant 'Ermosa' for fall and winter harvest. Red cabbages: 'Red Acre' stores well.

SUITED TO SMALL SPACES

Smooth-leaved 'Pixie' and early-maturing 'Red Jewel' are suitable for containers; crinkle-leaved 'Savoy Express' is compact.

CARROT

Daucus carota subsp. *sativus*
Half-hardy, cool-season biennial grown as
an annual

Eating carrots fresh from the garden is genuinely satisfy-ing. I always get a little thrill when I pull up the stems and find a carrot attached!

START Direct sow around the time of the last frost for your area, succession sowing every three weeks until mid-summer. Carrots tolerate light frosts, so you can harvest them well into the fall or winter in some climates. The seeds are tiny and can be hard to handle: sow them into a trench ¼ in. deep, or simply broadcast them into a con-tainer or bed and cover them with a shallow layer of fine soil. Carrots take up to three weeks to germinate; keep the soil moist during this time. Once the tops emerge, grad-ually begin thinning them until they are spaced 2 to 4 in. apart—eating the thinnings as you go.

GROW In full sun, in light, fluffy, moist soil in deeply dug beds. If your soil is rocky, compacted, or shallow, grow carrots in containers or raised beds instead. Carrots don't like overly rich or manured soils.

HARVEST Carrots can be harvested at any size, begin-ning with the baby carrots pulled during thinning. Gently pull them up by their tops, or use a garden fork or culti-vator to loosen them from the soil.

ADVICE If the tops of the roots begin to show, cover them with soil to prevent greening. Interplant carrots with alliums to confuse the carrot rust fly.

IN CONTAINERS Choose an appropriate (short) type and a container at least 10 in. deep.

PROBLEMS Carrot rust fly.

'Little Fingers' baby carrots are a great choice for container growing.

Carrot, *continued*

POPULAR SELECTIONS 'Royal Chantenay' is deep orange with good flavor. Grow unusual 'Atomic Red', 'Purple Haze', and 'Snow White' for the fun factor.

SUITED TO SMALL SPACES

'Thumbelina' is small and globe-shaped; 'Mignon' is a baby carrot. Both do well in containers.

CAULIFLOWER

Brassica oleracea var. *botrytis*
Half-hardy, cool-season annual

Cauliflower is a diva, demanding that conditions be just *so*, or refusing to produce. And it is a space hog that takes a long time to develop. Worth it? I don't think so, especially not in a small space, but cauliflower aficionados might disagree.

START Start indoors four to six weeks before last frost, or direct sow after soil has warmed up. Overwintering cauliflowers can be started in midsummer. Space transplants 24 in. apart.

GROW In full sun, in fertile, well-drained soil. Cauliflower dislikes heat and requires consistently moist soil to form heads. Inconsistent watering or insufficient soil nutrients will cause growth to slow or halt. To produce nice, white heads, choose self-blanching selections or use the outer leaves to cover the heads by securing with soft ties.

HARVEST Check heads frequently after they form; cut before the florets open.

ADVICE As with other brassicas, practice crop rotation to minimize the impact of pests and diseases.

IN CONTAINERS Choose containers at least 10 in. deep, and plant dwarf selections.

PROBLEMS Aphids, cabbage maggot, caterpillars, clubroot, cutworms, mildew.

POPULAR SELECTIONS 'Cheddar' forms orange heads; 'Graffiti' and 'Violet Queen' are purple. 'Verdant', a green-headed cauliflower, is compact and suited for containers.

CELERY AND CELERIAC

Apium graveolens and *A. graveolens* var. *rapaceum*
Half-hardy, cool-season biennials grown as annuals

Celery and its close cousin, celeriac (also known as celery root and knob celery), can be finicky to start from seed, requiring up to three weeks to germinate. To achieve the familiar mild taste of supermarket celery, blanching—protecting the growing stalks from sunlight—is required.

START Start seeds indoors ten to twelve weeks before last frost, sowing shallowly (the seeds require light to germinate) and keeping the soil consistently moist. Or skip the fuss and buy transplants; set them out after temperatures have warmed above 55°F. Space plants 12 in. apart.

GROW Celery grows best in full sun but tolerates afternoon shade. A heavy feeder, it prefers rich, fertile soil that is well drained and consistently moist. Amend soil with manure or a complete organic fertilizer prior to planting. Supplement with a liquid fertilizer throughout the growing season as needed.

HARVEST Harvest celery stalks individually throughout the growing season by removing one or two from the outside of the plant. Three weeks before harvesting, bundle each plant's tops together, and then either mound up soil around the stalks or wrap them in newspaper to protect them from the sun. Do not cover the leaves. Celeriac does not need to be blanched prior to harvesting, but do try to keep the root covered. Harvest when roots are 2 in. or more in diameter; simply pull up the root and remove the leaves.

ADVICE If blanching seems like too much trouble, choose a self-blanching type or try celeriac. The knobby root is delicious raw or cooked.

IN CONTAINERS Although they are not well suited for a small space, celery and celeriac will do fine in a half-barrel.

PROBLEMS Aphids, blight, caterpillars, cutworms, fusarium wilt.

POPULAR SELECTIONS Celery: 'Tall Utah 52-70' produces early and is resistant to disease; 'Golden Boy' is self-blanching. Celeriac: 'Giant Prague' is an heirloom cultivar that produces large bulbs.

CHARD

Beta vulgaris subsp. *cicla*
Half-hardy, cool-season biennial grown as an annual

Chard goes by a number of aliases, including Swiss chard, leaf beet, silverbeet, perpetual spinach, and spinach beet. As its common names suggest, it is related to spinach and, more closely, beets. Whatever you call it, chard deserves a place in your garden. It is gorgeous, nutritious, easy to grow, tolerates shade and frost, and is well suited for container growing.

START Direct sow in the garden at the time of last frost, and again in two to three weeks to prolong the harvest.

Sow again in late summer for a late fall or winter harvest. Sow densely and treat as a cut-and-come-again crop, or thin to 10 in. apart for full-sized plants.

GROW In full sun or part shade, in fertile, well-drained, consistently moist soil.

Like spinach, baby chard leaves can be eaten raw; steam or sauté mature leaf ribs.

Chard, continued

HARVEST Twist off outer stalks, or cut back the whole plant to the base when small for baby greens.

ADVICE Many beautiful selections of chard are available, with brightly colored ribs and deeply ruffled leaves. Even if you don't like its flavor, chard looks impressive in ornamental displays.

IN CONTAINERS Does well in containers at least 10 in. deep.

PROBLEMS Leaf miners, slugs.

POPULAR SELECTIONS 'Rhubarb Chard' has deep-red stems and is moderately winter-hardy.

SUITED TO SMALL SPACES

'Bright Lights' produces a mix of yellow, red, pink, and white stems.

CHERRY

Prunus spp.
Deciduous tree, hardy in zones 4–9

Cherries are one of the first fruits to ripen in the garden, which is reason enough to grow your own. Cherries are either sweet or sour (tart). The familiar sweet cherry loves the sun and is hardy only to −10°F; its midspring blooms can be damaged by frosts in some areas. The sour cherry, which is great for cooking and preserving, is hardier and easier to grow, surviving temperatures down to −30°F. Most sweet cherry trees will not self-pollinate, although a few self-pollinating selections are available. Sour cherries are self-pollinating.

START Purchase bare-root or container-grown trees. Transplant them from fall through spring. Spring is better for those in cold climates; warm-climate gardeners can plant in the fall.

GROW In full sun, in moist, well-drained soil. Amend soil with compost and bone meal prior to planting. Prune after flowering to maintain shape and size; in areas prone to bacterial canker, prune after harvesting. Cherries can be pruned into an open vase shape or espaliered against a sunny wall. Protect blossoms from late frosts by covering the tree with a light sheet or cloth if frost is imminent.

HARVEST From early to late summer, depending on the selection.

ADVICE Hang reflectors or cover trees with netting to protect developing fruit from marauding birds.

IN CONTAINERS Choose a dwarf tree and a large container or half-barrel at least 20 in. deep.

PROBLEMS Aphids, bacterial canker, birds, brown rot, caterpillars, powdery mildew.

POPULAR SELECTIONS Choose trees on a dwarfing rootstock, and talk to a reputable nursery for recommendations for your area. Sweet cherries (*Prunus avium*): 'Stella' is a small, self-pollinating tree that produces large, sweet cherries; 'Craig's Crimson' produces dark red, spicy, sweet cherries and is also self-pollinating. Sour (*P. cerasus*): 'North Star' is a dwarf, self-pollinating tree that is extremely hardy and productive; 'Montmorency' produces classic pie cherries on a hardy, self-pollinating tree.

CHILI PEPPER

see Pepper and hot pepper

CHINESE CABBAGE

Brassica rapa
Half-hardy, cool-season annual

The name Chinese cabbage is a bit vague, because it is applied to two distinctly different groups of leaf vegetables: *Brassica rapa* var. *pekinensis* forms upright, tightly packed heads and is often called Napa cabbage; *B. rapa* var. *chinensis* forms clusters of broad white stems and green leaves and is known as bok choy, pak choi, and Chinese chard.

START Direct sow in early spring or, in areas with mild winters, sow in midsummer for harvesting fall through spring. You can also start seeds indoors four weeks prior to the last frost.

GROW In well-drained, consistently moist, fertile soil amended with abundant organic matter. Chinese cabbage enjoys full sun when the weather is cool, but some shade is helpful in preventing bolting during warm weather. Add lime to acidic soils prior to planting and amend with manure or a complete organic fertilizer.

HARVEST Bok choy types can be harvested as a cut-and-come-again crop; snip off the whole plant just above soil level and it will resprout. Harvest outer leaves from full-sized plants, or cut the entire plant. Napa types should be harvested all at once. Both types are best harvested when young and tender.

ADVICE These vegetables are sensitive to day length and will bolt as the days get longer. Plan to start them early enough so that they are full-sized by midspring. In areas with cold springs, use black plastic mulch to warm the soil before planting.

IN CONTAINERS Choose compact selections and a container at least 10 in. deep.

PROBLEMS Aphids, cabbage maggot, caterpillars, clubroot, cutworms, mildew.

POPULAR SELECTIONS Napa types: 'Wa Wa Sai' is a baby Chinese cabbage well suited to container growing; 'Tenderheart' is slow to bolt. Bok choy: 'Mei Qing Choi' is compact and tender.

SUITED TO SMALL SPACES
Try 'Toy Choy', a miniature bok choy with dark green leaves.

CHIVES

Allium spp.
Perennial herb, hardy in zones 3–9

Attractive and easy to grow, chives are often planted to repel insect pests, particularly carrot rust fly. Their pretty globe-shaped, mauve flowers attract bees and other beneficial insects.

START Direct sow in early spring after the last frost. Sow seeds in clusters. Or purchase transplants and space 8 to 12 in. apart.

GROW In full to part sun, in moist, rich, well-drained soil.

HARVEST From spring through fall. Snip stems 2 in. above the base. Flowers can also be harvested and used in a salad.

ADVICE Chives make attractive edging plants for beds and filler plants for container groupings. Grow them with carrots, nightshades, and brassicas to ward off insect pests.

IN CONTAINERS Excellent in containers at least 4 in. deep.

Chives, *continued*

PROBLEMS Chives are fairly trouble free.

POPULAR SELECTIONS In addition to the common chive (*Allium schoenoprasum*), garlic chives (*A. tuberosum*), with their white flowers and strong garlic flavor, are also popular.

SUITED TO SMALL SPACES

Choose common chives (*Allium schoenoprasum*) for maximum versatility in the kitchen.

Lavender pom-poms help chives hold their own in an ornamental border.

CILANTRO (coriander)

Coriandrum sativum
Cool-season annual

Cilantro, also known as coriander, is popular in Mexican and Asian cooking. Often, the leaves are referred to as cilantro and the seeds are called coriander. The lacy plant produces tiny white flowers that attract beneficial insects.

START Direct sow in early spring around the time of the last frost, succession planting every two weeks to extend the harvest. You can also sow seeds in midsummer for a fall harvest. Space plants 4 to 6 in. apart.

GROW In full to part sun, in well-drained soil. Provide afternoon shade in hot summer climates.

HARVEST From spring through fall. Harvest leaves as needed; regular harvests will encourage new growth. Seeds can be collected in autumn as they ripen.

ADVICE Cilantro bolts easily in hot weather, so succession planting is essential if you want a continued harvest. Plant throughout your garden to attract beneficial insects.

IN CONTAINERS Excellent in containers at least 4 in. deep.

PROBLEMS Usually problem free.

POPULAR SELECTIONS Common cilantro is sold as *Coriandrum sativum*.

COLLARDS

Brassica oleracea var. *acephala*
Hardy, cool-season annual

These leafy, cold-hardy greens can be harvested all winter in all but the coldest climates.

START Best direct sown in late summer for harvesting in winter through spring, but they can also be sown in spring for a summer harvest. Space plants 12 to 18 in. apart.

GROW In full or part sun, in fertile, well-drained soil.

HARVEST Cut off lower leaves as needed.

ADVICE Although they prefer cool weather, collards are more heat-tolerant than many greens.

IN CONTAINERS Best in containers at least 12 in. deep.

PROBLEMS Aphids, caterpillars, clubroot, cutworms, mildew.

POPULAR SELECTIONS 'Champion' is a popular open-pollinated cultivar.

Collards like alkaline soil. Add lime to acid or neutral soil three weeks before planting.

CORN

Zea mays
Tender, warm-season grass

You will never taste corn as good as the cobs you eat immediately after harvesting them. Unfortunately, corn, also known as maize, is not suited to growing in very small spaces.

START Direct sow in late spring after soil has warmed to at least 60°F. Corn needs a long, hot growing season to do well. Because corn is wind-pollinated, it is best planted in blocks of at least four rows. Space plants to 10 to 18 in. apart.

GROW In full sun, in fertile, consistently moist, well-drained soil. Corn is a heavy feeder, so amend the soil with manure or compost before planting.

HARVEST After the silks on the cobs turn brown, peek inside and pinch a kernel; if it sprays a milky juice, it's ready for harvest. Twist the cobs off the stalks.

ADVICE New hybrids stay sweeter longer—look for seeds marked Supersweet (Sh2) or Sugar Enhanced (SE). Different varieties of corn will cross-pollinate readily, making them inedible. Grow only one type at a time, or plant selections that mature at different times. Try growing popcorn: dry the cobs indoors prior to popping.

IN CONTAINERS Not suited to container growing.

PROBLEMS Aphids, caterpillars, cutworms, flea beetles, raccoons, squirrels, wilt, wireworms.

POPULAR SELECTIONS 'Early Sunglow' matures quickly and grows in cooler weather; 'Peaches and Cream' is a bicolored cultivar. 'Strawberry' popcorn produces deep-red kernels that turn white when popped.

CUCUMBER

Cucumis sativus
Tender, warm-season annual

Usually categorized as slicers or picklers, cucumbers are easy to grow and do well in containers. Grow climbers up a trellis or teepee, or choose a bush type for compact container growing.

START Start indoors four weeks before last frost, or direct sow after the soil has warmed. Cucurbits dislike

Save space by growing vining cucumber vertically.

being moved, so if you are seeding indoors, use a newspaper or other biodegradable pot to avoid disturbing the roots when transplanting.

GROW In full sun, in moist, fertile, well-drained soil. Cucumbers need warm weather to produce; use black plastic mulch or cloches to warm the soil in cool climates. Amend soil with compost prior to planting. Keep the soil consistently moist, especially after fruit has started forming; dry soil can cause bitterness. Avoid getting water on the leaves; it encourages mildew.

HARVEST Pickling cucumbers are best harvested when young and small; slicing cucumbers can be harvested at 6 to 8 in. long. Harvest frequently to encourage greater production.

ADVICE Cucumbers available for home growing go well beyond the straight green cukes found in supermarkets. If pollinators are scarce, you can hand-pollinate cucumbers by transferring pollen from the center of the male flower (held on a stem) to the center of a female flower (with a tiny fruit at its base). Use a small paintbrush or cotton swab, or pick the male flower, remove the petals, and brush it onto the female flower.

IN CONTAINERS Bush cucumbers are well suited to containers at least 10 in. deep.

PROBLEMS Aphids, cucumber beetles, flea beetles, mildew, mosaic virus, squash vine borers, wilt, whitefly.

POPULAR SELECTIONS 'Salad Bush' is a good slicing cucumber that is suited to containers; 'Marketmore' is a popular standard green slicer. 'Patio Pickles' is a prolific pickling cultivar suited to container growing. Try a pale-skinned apple type, or an Armenian cucumber, which can grow up to 3 ft. long.

SUITED TO SMALL SPACES

I particularly like heirloom 'Lemon' as a slicing cucumber.

CURRANT AND GOOSEBERRY

Ribes spp.
Deciduous perennial shrubs, hardy in zones 3–9

Red, white, and black currants, along with gooseberries and jostaberries (a cross between gooseberry and black currant), are deciduous berry-producing shrubs that grow well in areas with cold winters and mild summers. Gooseberries can grow to be quite large; however, they can also be trained as a standard (with one main stem). Currants and gooseberries can also be espaliered against a wall or fence.

START Purchase bare-root or container-grown plants, or take a cutting from a friend's plant—they root easily. Transplant from fall through early spring. Spring is better for those in cold climates; gardeners in warm climates can plant in the fall. Space currants and gooseberries at least 4 ft. apart.

GROW In full or part sun, in moist, rich, well-drained soil. Prune in late summer or early spring, removing canes that are more than a couple of years old for black currants; in their third year or older for red and white currants and gooseberries. Train a gooseberry into a standard by selecting a leader (main stem) and summer pruning any side branches to the fifth set of leaves.

HARVEST From midsummer to late summer, depending on the type.

ADVICE Harvest up to half of the crop early in the season to allow the remaining fruit to grow larger and sweeter. Use the first batch of berries for cooking.

Currants, *continued*

IN CONTAINERS Suitable for containers at least 14 in. deep.

PROBLEMS Aphids, birds, blight, mildew, rust.

POPULAR SELECTIONS Currants (*Ribes* spp.): 'Ben Sarek' is a prolific dwarf black currant; 'White Imperial' produces sweet white currants on a small shrub; 'Viking' is a red currant cultivar that is high-yielding and resistant to mildew and rust. Gooseberries (*R. uva-crispa*): 'Oregon Champion' is an older cultivar that produces rosy pink fruit; 'Invicta' produces large, green fruits on a sprawling shrub.

DILL

Anethum graveolens
Cool-season annual

Dill is a tall-growing, feathery-foliaged herb that produces lovely umbrella-shaped flowers. The leaves are often used in fish dishes, and the seeds are used in pickling.

START Direct sow in early spring around the time of last frost. Space plants 12 in. apart.

GROW In full sun in a sheltered location, in moist, well-drained soil. Do not grow near fennel if you want to use the seeds; the plants will cross-pollinate readily and the seeds of both will be affected.

HARVEST Pick leaves as needed. Harvest seed heads in late summer after they have started to dry; place them in a paper bag until they are fully dry.

ADVICE Dill is a great asset to the edible garden; it attracts beneficial insects while repelling a number of pests. Plant with lettuces, brassicas, and alliums.

IN CONTAINERS Plant in a container of at least 10 in. deep.

PROBLEMS Rarely suffers from pests or diseases.

POPULAR SELECTIONS 'Long Island Mammoth', one of the most commonly grown cultivars, is a tall plant with large flowers.

SUITED TO SMALL SPACES

'Fernleaf Dill' is a dwarf cultivar that grows to 18 in. tall and grows well in containers.

EGGPLANT

Solanum melongena
Tender, warm-season perennial grown as an annual

Eggplants, also known as aubergines, can be difficult to grow in areas with short or cool summers. However, they do wonderfully in containers and are truly beautiful plants.

START Start seeds indoors five to eight weeks before the last frost and transplant into the garden after daytime temperatures are regularly above 70°F. Space plants 2 ft. apart.

GROW Eggplants need full sun and a sheltered location. Soil should be moist, fertile, and well drained; amend with compost or manure prior to planting. Use black plastic mulch, cloches, or row covers to raise the soil temperature.

HARVEST Cut fruits from the plant with a sharp knife while they are still glossy.

ADVICE Choose fast-maturing eggplants in areas with shorter summers. Some may require staking to support heavy fruit.

Harvest eggplant early and often to encourage greater production.

Eggplant, *continued*

IN CONTAINERS Eggplants thrive in containers at least 10 in. deep.

PROBLEMS Aphids, blight, cutworms, flea beetles, leafhoppers, potato beetles, white fly, wilt.

POPULAR SELECTIONS 'Dusky' produces large purple fruit even in cooler summers.

SUITED TO SMALL SPACES

'Fairy Tale' is a quick-maturing, pink-and-white-striped cultivar ideal for containers.

FENNEL AND FLORENCE FENNEL

Foeniculum vulgare
Cool-season perennial often grown as an annual, hardy to zone 6

Two types of fennel are commonly grown. The first, sometimes called common fennel, is an herb grown for its seeds and feathery leaves; the second, known as Florence or bulb fennel, is grown for its edible bulb, which is used as a vegetable. Both are eye-catching plants that attract beneficial insects.

START Start indoors six weeks before the last frost, direct sow at the time of the last frost, or sow in midsummer for a fall harvest. Fennel dislikes being moved, so if you sow indoors, use a newspaper or other biodegradable pot to avoid disturbing the roots when transplanting.

GROW In full sun, in moist, well-drained soil, and a sheltered position. Fennel quickly bolts in hot weather, so it does best when it matures in spring or fall. Consistent moisture can also prevent bolting; apply a mulch to prevent evaporation. Space plants 12 in. apart. Florence fennel will be more tender if you mound up mulch around the base. Do not grow near dill if you want to use the seeds; the plants will cross-pollinate readily and the seeds of both will be affected.

HARVEST Cut leaves as needed. Bulbs can be harvested after the base has thickened. Seeds can be collected and saved in late summer or fall by clipping off seed heads and placing them in paper bags.

ADVICE
Fennel produces attractive, fernlike fronds that look right at home in an ornamental bed or border.

IN CONTAINERS Choose containers at least 12 in. deep.

PROBLEMS Fennel is usually free of problems.

POPULAR SELECTIONS Florence fennel (*Foeniculum vulgare* var. *azoricum*): 'Selma Fino' is bolt resistant; 'Victorio' is a good choice for overwintering. Common fennel (*F. vulgare* var. *dulce*) is very cold hardy.

FIG

Ficus carica
Deciduous tree, hardy in zones 6–11

With their deeply lobed leaves and deliciously Mediterranean fruit, fig trees are excellent additions to any garden. Unchecked, they can grow to 30 ft. tall; however, they can be kept small by pruning or by growing them in containers. In fact, figs are an excellent choice for container growing—which also makes it easier to move them indoors in cold winters.

START Purchase bare-root or container-grown plants. Transplant trees from fall through early spring. Spring is better for those in cold climates; gardeners in warm climates can plant in the fall.

GROW In full sun, in a warm, sheltered location. In areas with cool summers, plant in front of a light-colored, sunny wall, which will retain and reflect warmth. Soil should be rich in organic matter, moist, and well drained. Prune into an open-center shape or espalier. Mulch thickly with leaves or straw in winter to protect shallow-growing roots. If temperatures are expected to drop below the hardiness rating for your particular type of fig, bundle and tie the branches together and wrap them with burlap, or move container-grown trees indoors.

HARVEST Figs often produce two crops—the first, called the breba crop, is produced in spring on last season's growth; the second, or main crop, is produced in the fall on new growth. Fruit is ripe when it is soft and ready to drop.

ADVICE Figs actually benefit from having their roots constrained—container growing improves both the quality and quantity of fruit. (Just remember that container growing makes plants less cold tolerant.)

IN CONTAINERS Excellent in containers at least 18 in. deep.

PROBLEMS Birds.

POPULAR SELECTIONS 'King' produces well in cool, coastal areas; 'Hardy Chicago' is the best choice for areas with cold winters.

SUITED TO SMALL SPACES

'Brown Turkey' thrives in my Pacific Northwest garden, forming a small tree that produces deep purple fruit.

Fig trees suit small spaces; they're self-fertile so you only need one.

GARLIC

Allium sativum
Perennial bulb, hardy in zones 3–11

Didn't get your winter garden planted? There is still time for garlic. Garlic is most often planted in fall and harvested the following summer, although a small harvest can usually be achieved through early spring planting. In addition to its bulb, which is a kitchen mainstay, garlic's scape, or central stalk, is also edible. Two crops in one!

START Choose the largest cloves from heads bought from a farmers' market or seed company. Separate the cloves just prior to planting. Plant in autumn just prior to the first frost by sowing individual cloves, pointy end up, 1 to 2 in. deep and 4 to 6 in. apart. Tighter spacing will produce more, but smaller, bulbs.

GROW In full sun, in fertile, well-drained soil. Keep the soil moist; mulch to conserve moisture, protect against temperature extremes, and reduce weeds.

HARVEST Carefully dig the bulbs in summer or autumn, when the bottom three or four leaves are dead. Cure them by hanging in a cool, well-ventilated place until the skins are dry.

ADVICE Hardneck garlic produces a looping central stalk called a scape, which can be harvested and eaten. Scapes are delicious steamed or stir-fried, and cutting them back actually helps produce a larger bulb.

IN CONTAINERS Garlic does well even in small containers (6 in. deep), but they are happier in large containers or raised beds.

PROBLEMS Rot, rust.

POPULAR SELECTIONS Garlic is divided into hardneck and softneck types. Hardneck cultivars such as 'Russian Red', 'Leningrad', and 'Spanish Roja' are best for cold-climate areas; softneck cultivars such as 'Inchelium Red' and 'Susanville' are the best choices for areas with mild winters.

GRAPE

Vitis spp. (*Vitaceae*)
Perennial vine, hardy in zones 3–9

You may not have room for your own personal vineyard, but you can cultivate *terroir* with just one grapevine growing against a sunny wall, up a railing, or along a fence. Grapes are perennial vines that require only a few things: a sunny location, excellent drainage, annual pruning, and time. They may not produce a full crop until their fifth year. In the meantime, harvest what you can and make dolmades with the young grape leaves.

START Buy bare-root vines for planting during late winter or early spring. Plant at the base of a trellis, arbor, porch, or other vertical structure that can be used for support.

GROW In full or part sun, in a sunny location. In areas with cool summers, a light-colored, sunny wall can help to generate warmth. Soil should be moist and well drained, but it need not be overly rich. Grapes produce fruit on the current year's growth, so pruning is necessary to promote new growth from old wood. Prune the vine to fit your space, making sure to prune enough to stimulate growth and provide air circulation, or you can follow a more formal program of shaping your vine. Traditionally, grapevines are trained to a central trunk with two sets of arms that produce short, fruiting spurs. Each winter, the dormant shoots of that year's new growth are cut back to two buds. Different types of grapes require different types of pruning techniques—ask the nursery which is best for your grape.

HARVEST Summer to late fall, depending on type. Cut bunches of ripe grapes from the vines with pruning shears.

ADVICE Grapevines make gorgeous living walls and roofs. Use them to shade a sweltering patio or beautify an ugly fence or wall.

IN CONTAINERS Although grapes grown in ground do not mind poor soil, container-grown grapes respond well to fertilizing with liquid seaweed, wood ashes, and bone meal each spring. They prefer a large container at least 18 in. deep.

PROBLEMS Aphids, canker, mildew.

POPULAR SELECTIONS 'Concord' is a hardy, multi-purpose blue-black grape; 'Interlaken' produces seedless green grapes and is good for areas with cool or short summers; 'Thompson' is a classic green seedless grape that is suited to mild winters and hot summers. Purpleleaf grape (*Vitis vinifera* 'Purpurea'), with its stunning deep purple foliage, is sold mainly as an ornamental, but its fruit is edible.

Fresh, dried, or juiced, grapes are delicious and a good fruiting vine.

KALE

Brassica oleracea var. *acephala*
Hardy, cool-season biennial grown as an annual

If you are not already a fan of kale, give it a chance. Kale is an attractive, frost-tolerant plant and is easy to grow in rich soil.

START Direct sow in early spring for a summer harvest or in midsummer for harvesting winter through spring. Sow spring crops densely and treat as a cut-and-come-again vegetable, or thin to 12 to 18 in. apart for full-sized plants.

GROW In full or part sun, in fertile, well-drained soil. Amend acidic soils with lime prior to planting, and add compost or manure to all soils. In containers, fertilize with a nitrogen-rich liquid fertilizer during the growing season.

HARVEST Harvest lower leaves as needed, or cut back the plant when it is 2 to 3 in. tall, and eat the baby greens. The youngest leaves are most tender.

ADVICE Kale will overwinter in all but the coldest climates. Harvest leaves all winter long, and eat the flowers that emerge in spring. All kales make excellent additions to ornamental edible gardens.

Kale, *continued*

IN CONTAINERS Best in containers at least 10 in. deep.

PROBLEMS Aphids, caterpillars, clubroot, cutworms, leaf miners, mildew.

POPULAR SELECTIONS Beautiful 'Lacinato' (Black Tuscan) kale has large, sword-shaped, blue-green leaves; 'Rainbow Lacinato' is a multicolored cross between 'Lacinato' and super-hardy 'Redbor'; 'Red Russian' has sawtooth leaves with red veins; 'Redbor' is a deeply ruffled purple cultivar.

KOHLRABI

Brassica oleracea var. *gongylodes*
Hardy, cool-season biennial grown as an annual

This odd-looking vegetable makes a good succession crop and tolerates frost.

START Sow seeds directly in the garden around the time of last frost. Succession sow every two weeks thereafter until late spring; sow again in late summer for a fall crop. Space plants 4 in. apart.

GROW In full sun, in fertile, moist soil. Amend soil with compost or manure and a complete organic fertilizer before planting. Kohlrabi grown in hot conditions will produce mediocre bulbs.

HARVEST Once the bulbs are golf ball–sized, harvest them quickly; they can become woody if they are left in the ground. Pull up the root and discard the leaves. Peel the root before eating.

ADVICE Grow white, green, and purple selections for a pretty display.

IN CONTAINERS Good even in small containers (6 in. deep).

PROBLEMS Aphids, caterpillars, clubroot, cutworms, leaf miners, mildew.

POPULAR SELECTIONS 'Purple Vienna' and 'White Vienna' are popular open-pollinated cultivars; 'Gigante' produces large bulbs that resist turning woody.

Kohlrabi bulbs stay tender longer in cool weather; to avoid woodiness, sow in late summer.

LEEK

Allium porrum
Hardy, cool-season biennial grown as an annual

Leeks are one of the standouts of the winter garden, and, like all alliums, they make good companions to many other crops.

START In areas with cold winters, start leeks indoors six to ten weeks before the last frost, or purchase transplants and plant them out after the last frost. In areas with mild winters, plant leeks in the late summer for harvesting the following spring. Set transplants into a furrow (shallow ditch) or hole about 6 in. deep. Bury plants to just below the first leaf, and water in. The hole will fill with soil over time. This technique blanches the bottom of the stalk, giving it its white color and mild flavor.

GROW In full sun, in moist, fertile, well-drained soil. Continue to mound up soil around the stalks during the growing season to ensure blanching.

HARVEST Dig carefully when stems are about ½ in. thick or larger. Many leeks are frost hardy, so you can leave them in the ground; if the ground isn't frozen, you can harvest them throughout the winter.

ADVICE Choose "baby" leeks for container growing.

IN CONTAINERS Best in containers at least 10 in. deep.

PROBLEMS Mildew, rot, rust.

POPULAR SELECTIONS 'King Richard' produces baby leeks early in the season; 'Bandit' is winter-hardy.

LETTUCE AND SALAD GREENS

Various species
Half-hardy, cool-season annuals and perennials

Lettuce and other salad greens make ideal small-space edibles. Space-efficient, fast-maturing, attractive, and easy to grow, these leafy greens can keep you in salad almost year-round. Arugula, chervil, chicory, corn salad (also known as mâche or lamb's lettuce), cress, endive, escarole, miner's lettuce, radicchio, and sorrel are all popular salad greens that are often sold as a mesclun mix—a blend of greens meant to be harvested young as a cut-and-come-again crop.

True lettuce—*Lactuca sativa*—includes easy-to-grow leaf (or loose-leaf) lettuce, which produces clusters of tender leaves that may be green, red, bronze, or speckled; creamy butterhead or bibb lettuce, which forms a loose head; crisphead lettuce, which is slow growing and forms a tight head; and romaine or cos lettuce, which produces a head with broad, upright leaves.

START Direct sow in the garden around the time of last frost, succession planting every two to three weeks for an extended harvest. Plant in late summer for a fall harvest, protecting with cloches or cold frames if necessary. Scatter seeds over moistened soil. For loose-leaf types, thin to 8 in. apart. You can eat the thinnings or treat as a cut-and-come-again crop. Heading lettuces should be thinned to about 12 in. apart.

GROW In full sun to part shade, in fertile, moist, well-drained soil. Lettuce and salad greens grow best in cool weather; warm weather causes lettuce to bolt or acquire a bitter taste. Provide plenty of water and protection from

Lettuces of different colors and shapes create a pretty plot—and plate.

Lettuce, *continued*

the sun during the hot summer months. Grow lettuces in the shade of taller plants, under a vine-covered arbor, or in a container that can be moved into shade. Fertilize container-grown plants with a nitrogen-rich fertilizer throughout the growing season.

HARVEST Harvest the outer leaves of loose-leaf lettuces and greens as needed, or cut just above the ground for a cut-and-come-again crop. Harvest heading lettuces as soon as the head is full.

ADVICE Try a variety of salad greens by planting a blend of greens such as arugula, chervil, endive, and mizuna—many of which are found in mesclun mixes. These varieties are more cold tolerant than true lettuce, and can be planted up to a month before last frost.

IN CONTAINERS Good even in small containers (6 in. deep).

PROBLEMS Leaf miners, slugs.

POPULAR SELECTIONS Butterhead: 'Buttercrunch' tolerates heat; 'Tom Thumb' is compact. Leaf lettuce: Oakleaf lettuce is frilly and tender. Romaine: 'Little Gem' is compact; 'Rouge d'Hiver' is a cold-tolerant heirloom that forms a loose head. Crisphead: 'Summertime' is a classic iceberg lettuce. Salad greens: peppery arugula and mild corn salad (mâche) tolerate frost; endive and radicchio really perk up salads.

SUITED TO SMALL SPACES

Butterhead cultivar 'Garden Babies' was born for containers. I also like leaf lettuce varieties 'Green Deer Tongue', which is an heirloom, and 'Red Sails', which tolerates heat and is very pretty.

MELON

Cucumis melo and *Citrullus lanatus*
Warm-season annual vines

Watermelon, cantaloupe, and honeydew melons need long, warm summers to produce well. Given that, plus abundant water and rich soil, they will reward you with sweet, juicy fruit. Cantaloupe and honeydew mature earlier and are easier to grow in areas with short growing seasons.

START Start indoors midspring and transplant outdoors after daytime temperatures are regularly above 68°F. Space plants 3 to 4 ft. apart, or plant one per large container. Sowing in raised beds or hills (mounded soil) is popular because this improves drainage.

GROW In full sun and a warm, sheltered location. Soil should be moist, fertile, and well drained. Amend with compost or manure prior to planting. A handful of bone meal will provide the calcium needed for fruit development. In areas with mild summers, use black plastic mulch, cloches, or row covers to raise the soil temperature. Water regularly, avoiding the leaves; erratic watering will cause fruit to fail.

HARVEST In late summer. Allow melons to ripen fully on the vine. Cantaloupe and honeydew melons will easily come away from the stem when ripe; watermelon will sound hollow when tapped.

ADVICE Choose earlier maturing selections in areas with shorter summers. Support heavy, trellis-grown fruits with netting; you can create melon slings from old pantyhose. Ensure good fruit production in areas where few native pollinators exist by hand-pollinating flowers.

IN CONTAINERS Good in large containers at least 12 in. deep.

Melon, *continued*

PROBLEMS Aphids, cucumber beetles, mildew.

POPULAR SELECTIONS Honeydew (*Cucumis melo* var. *inodorus*): 'Earli Dew' is early ripening and disease resistant. Cantaloupe (*C. melo* var. *cantalupensis*): 'Ambrosia' is popular for its sweet flavor and scent. Watermelon (*Citrullus lanatus*): 'Northern Sweet' ripens early and was developed for areas with short summers; 'Yellow Doll' is a yellow-fleshed bush type that is good for small spaces.

MESCLUN

see Lettuce and salad greens

MINT

Mentha spp.
Perennial herb, hardy in zones 3–11

Whether you're into mojitos or herbal tea, fresh mint comes in handy. I recommend growing mint if you are feeling defeated or otherwise skeptical about gardening: it is one of the easiest edibles to grow. In fact, mint is so robust that it is often considered invasive. Best grow it in a pot to contain its spreading roots.

START Take a cutting from a friend's plant or purchase a plant from a nursery.

The key to melon-growing success: plenty of water, heat, and sun.

GROW In part sun, in moist, well-drained soil. Pinch back tips regularly to encourage bushy growth.

HARVEST Harvest regularly, pinching out the tips of the stems or snipping whole stems back to soil level. Mint is easily dried for later use.

ADVICE Mint's vigorously spreading roots can quickly outgrow a container. To keep mint healthy, lift and divide the plant each year. In addition to using mint for culinary purposes, it also makes a great filler for bouquets; fresh-cut mint smells divine.

IN CONTAINERS Needs a container at least 8 in. deep.

PROBLEMS Rust, wilt.

POPULAR SELECTIONS Spearmint (*Mentha spicata*) and peppermint (*M. piperita*) are popular, but also try lemon mint, apple mint, pineapple mint, and even chocolate mint—the list is seemingly endless.

MUSTARD GREENS

see Asian greens

OKRA

Abelmoschus esculentus
Tender, warm-season annual

Okra grows best in areas with long, hot summers. It is an attractive, tropical-looking plant that does well in containers.

START Indoors four to eight weeks before the last frost, soaking the seeds for twenty-four hours prior to sowing. Transplant outside after temperatures are steadily above 70°F, spacing plants 2 ft. apart.

GROW In full sun, in a sheltered position, in fertile, well-drained soil.

HARVEST Harvest the pods when they are 2 to 4 in. long, wearing gloves to protect yourself from the tiny spines. Harvest frequently to encourage production.

ADVICE In cooler climates, place plants near a heat trap such as a concrete wall. Move container-grown plants indoors if the weather turns cold.

IN CONTAINERS Choose containers at least 10 in. deep.

PROBLEMS Aphids, mildew, mites.

POPULAR SELECTIONS 'Cajun Delight' is early and high-yielding; 'Red Burgundy' has scarlet stalks and pods.

ONION, SCALLION, AND SHALLOT

Allium spp.
Hardy, cool-season bulbs

Onions of all types are pantry staples, and they are equally useful in the garden. They repel pests, and many are good choices for the winter garden.

START Onions are started from seeds or from dormant bulbs called sets. Scallions, also known as green or bunching onions, are best started from seed; bulb onions and shallots can be grown from sets or seeds. Sets give you a head start on the growing season, but seeds often yield larger bulbs. Start seeds indoors six to eight weeks prior to last frost, or direct sow at that time. Plant

Onions, continued

scallions 1 to 2 in. apart, and plant bulb onions and shallots 4 to 8 in. apart.

GROW In full sun, in fertile, well-drained soil. Amend soil with compost and keep well watered.

HARVEST As needed throughout the growing season. Bulb onions and shallots are mature when their leaves begin to yellow and dry. If you plan to store the bulbs, push over any leaves that are still standing, wait a week, and then dig them up. Allow them to dry in a cool, dry spot for a week before storing.

ADVICE Choose bulb onions based on your latitude: northern gardeners should choose long-day onions, while short-day onions do well in the South.

IN CONTAINERS Scallions and shallots do well even in small containers (6 in. deep); bulb onions require more space.

PROBLEMS Mildew, rot.

POPULAR SELECTIONS Bulb onions: 'Ailsa Craig' produces large yellow bulbs and is day-length neutral; 'Walla Walla' is a mild, sweet, overwintering long-day cultivar. Shallots: 'Ambition' produces large, long-keeping bulbs. Scallions: 'Evergreen' is winter hardy.

Maturing bulb onions emerge from the soil. It's cool. Just leave them be.

OREGANO AND MARJORAM

Origanum spp.
Perennial herbs, hardy in zones 5–11

These closely related herbs are essential in the cuisines of many Mediterranean cultures. Marjoram is the milder and sweeter of the two, but it is does not tolerate frost. In areas with cold winters, marjoram can be treated as an annual or brought indoors to overwinter.

START Start seeds indoors four to six weeks prior to last frost, or direct sow after soil has warmed. Seeds can be slow to germinate, so it is more common to purchase transplants. Space plants 10 to 12 in. apart.

GROW In full sun or part shade, in well-drained soil; or indoors on a sunny window sill. Pinch back growing tips to encourage bushy growth.

HARVEST Harvest regularly, pinching out the tips of the stems or snipping whole stems to soil level. Oregano and marjoram are easily dried for later use.

ADVICE The flavor of oregano is often considered better when dried. Cut whole stems prior to flowering and hang them in a cool, dry place. Once the leaves are dry and almost brittle, remove the leaves from the stems and store them in a glass jar.

IN CONTAINERS Good in containers at least 6 in. deep.

PROBLEMS Oregano and marjoram rarely suffer from pests or diseases.

POPULAR SELECTIONS Sweet marjoram is often sold as *Origanum marjorana*. Also try golden oregano (*O. vulgare* 'Aureum') for its attractive golden foliage.

SUITED TO SMALL SPACES

Chefs consider Greek oregano, *Origanum vulgare* subsp. *hirtum*, best for cooking.

ORIENTAL CABBAGE

see Chinese cabbage

PAK CHOI

see Chinese cabbage

PARSLEY

Petroselinum crispum
Biennial herb, usually grown as an annual

Flat-leaved Italian parsley is possibly the most useful herb to have in the garden; I never seem to grow enough. Parsley is a biennial, overwintering in areas with mild winters and reviving in spring to produce seed. For this reason, it is usually grown as an annual, although it readily self-sows, so it is not always necessary to buy new plants or seeds each year.

START Direct sow in spring after last frost, or start seeds indoors two to three weeks prior. Soak seeds overnight before sowing. Parsley resents having its roots disturbed and transplants easiest when it is still young. Seeds can take up to three weeks to germinate, so many gardeners purchase transplants. Space plants 6 to 8 in. apart.

GROW In full sun or part shade, in rich, moist, well-drained soil.

HARVEST Pick individual stems from the outside of the plant as needed.

ADVICE Grow parsley as a companion to tomatoes and to attract beneficial insects.

IN CONTAINERS Good in containers at least 8 in. deep.

PROBLEMS Rarely suffers from pests or diseases.

POPULAR SELECTIONS Curly-leaved parsley (*Petroselinum crispum*) is attractive in containers and on the plate.

SUITED TO SMALL SPACES

Try flat-leaved Italian parsley (*Petroselinum crispum* var. *neapolitanum*) for cooking.

PARSNIP

Pastinaca sativa
Hardy, cool-season biennial grown as an annual

These carrot relatives taste sweeter after being touched by frost; roasting the roots makes them even sweeter.

START Direct sow in early spring, or sow in midsummer for winter harvesting. Parsnip seed does not store well, and even good seed has a low germination rate. Sow two to three seeds for every plant you want to grow. Parsnips take up to three weeks to germinate; keep the soil moist during this time. Once the tops emerge, gradually begin spacing them until they are 3 to 4 in. apart.

GROW In full or part sun. Like carrots, parsnips like light, fluffy soil in deeply dug beds. Some parsnips can have roots up to 18 in. long; remove rocks and break up soil to this depth to allow them room to develop.

HARVEST Parsnips can be dug at any size, but they taste better after a frost. Harvest all winter long, mulching with straw in areas with cold winters. Parsnips also store well.

ADVICE Interplant with quick-maturing radishes or lettuce to mark your planting site and use space efficiently.

IN CONTAINERS Traditional deep-rooted parsnips are not suited to containers less than 18 in. deep.

PROBLEMS Carrot rust fly, gophers.

POPULAR SELECTIONS 'Dagger' is a miniature hybrid suited for container growing; 'Harris Model' has sweet, tender roots.

Harvest parsnips as needed all winter long.

PEACH AND NECTARINE

Prunus persica
Deciduous tree, hardy in zones 4–9

Peaches and nectarines love cold winters and long, hot, dry summers. Dwarf trees grow well in large containers and, with their pretty spring flowers, are a good choice for a small patio.

START Bare-root or container-grown trees can be transplanted from fall through spring. Spring is better for those in cold climates; gardeners in warm climates can plant in the fall.

GROW In full sun, in a warm location sheltered from early spring frosts (which can destroy the blossoms). Soil should be rich and well drained. Prune into an open vase shape or espalier. Peaches and nectarines produce fruit on new growth, so it is important to prune annually. Thin the fruits in early summer when they are small, leaving 8 to 10 in. between fruits; even more when the tree is young.

HARVEST In midsummer to late summer, depending on type. Ripe fruits will come away from the branch easily with a slight twist.

ADVICE Peaches and nectarines are prone to fungal diseases promoted by wet foliage. In rainy climates, grow them in a container under an awning or porch until the heaviest of the spring rains have passed, or espalier a tree against a sunny wall under an overhang. Spray with horticultural oil and remove any leaves that show signs of infection to help combat disease.

IN CONTAINERS Good in containers at least 20 in. deep.

PROBLEMS Brown rot, peach leaf curl.

POPULAR SELECTIONS Choose trees on a dwarfing rootstock. Peaches: 'Bonanza' is a genetic dwarf freestone peach that grows to 6 ft.; 'Red Haven' is an early-ripening, freestone peach that is resistant to leaf curl. Nectarines: 'Necta Zee' is a dwarf tree that produces yellow-fleshed freestone fruit and showy flowers; 'Arctic Glo' is an early-ripening cultivar suited to areas with mild winters.

PEAR

Pyrus spp.
Deciduous tree, hardy in zones 4–9

With their pretty white blossoms, pears make a beautiful specimen tree. Their growing requirements are similar to those of apples, to which they are related. Like apples, most pears will not self-pollinate, so plant at least two different types of pears or plant a tree with several types of pears grafted onto it.

Until established, pears need supplemental watering during dry spells.

Pear, *continued*

START Bare-root or container-grown trees can be transplanted from fall through spring. Spring is better in climates with cold winters; in areas with milder winters, trees can be planted in the fall.

GROW In full sun, in moist, well-drained soil. Prune into an open, vase shape or espalier. Thinning is not required.

HARVEST Unlike most fruits, pears should be picked prior to ripening or they will spoil. Harvest when the fruit is well shaped but still too firm to eat. Place in a cool location to ripen.

ADVICE Fire blight is a significant problem in some areas. Choose resistant types if the disease is common in your region.

IN CONTAINERS Choose a dwarfing tree and a large container or half-barrel at least 24 in. deep.

PROBLEMS Aphids, codling moth, fire blight, powdery mildew, scab.

POPULAR SELECTIONS Choose trees on a dwarfing rootstock such as Quince C. 'Comice' and 'Conference' are russeted dessert pears that are available in dwarf and cordon forms; 'Moonglow' is disease resistant with mild flavor. Also look for Asian pears (*Pyrus serotina*).

PEAS

Pisum sativum
Cool-season annual

Peas are an ideal home garden crop in many ways: they taste best eaten fresh off the vine; they sprout even in cold weather, making them one of the earliest spring crops; and the climbing types make attractive screens. The only drawback for the small-space grower is that you need several plants to harvest any kind of proper meal. Shelling peas are removed from the pod before eating. Snap peas are eaten whole in the pod. Snow peas are eaten as immature, nearly seedless pods. They are all grown in the same way.

START Direct sow in late winter to early spring, spacing seeds 2 in. apart. Sow again three weeks later to extend the harvest, and again in midsummer for a fall crop. Use a legume inoculant on seeds prior to planting or in the planting hole to encourage healthy growth.

GROW In full or part sun, in moist, well-drained soil. Amend with compost prior to planting. Tall, climbing peas should be trellised, but shorter plants can trail over the sides of a container.

HARVEST Harvest young, tender pods frequently to encourage production. Shelling peas should be harvested when the seeds are full-sized but not yet bulging; snow and snap peas can be harvested just as the seeds start to form.

ADVICE If you cannot decide between shelling and edible pod peas, grow sugar snap peas, which can be harvested young and eaten whole or shelled later when the peas have swelled.

IN CONTAINERS Best in containers at least 8 in. deep.

PROBLEMS Powdery mildew, rot.

POPULAR SELECTIONS Shelling: 'Alderman' (or 'Tall Telephone') is exceptionally tall and produces huge pods; 'Lincoln' is a low-growing cultivar that is powdery mildew–resistant. Snap: 'Sugar Lace' is low growing and early. Snow: 'Oregon Giant' remains tender even when large; 'Kelvedon Wonder' is productive and low growing.

SUITED TO SMALL SPACES

'Super Sugar Snap' is crunchy and sweet. Another snap I like is 'Sugar Ann', which is low growing and early.

PEPPER AND HOT PEPPER

Capsicum annuum
Tender, warm-season perennials grown as annuals

Peppers and hot peppers can be found in almost every color of the rainbow and are fantastic container crops. The main issue with their cultivation is sun and heat: peppers require a very warm summer to produce well. Perhaps surprisingly, gardeners in areas with mild or cool summers often have more success with hot peppers than with sweet peppers.

START Buy transplants from a nursery or sow indoors six to eight weeks prior to the last frost. Transplant seedlings into a larger container and harden off before planting them outdoors in late spring or early summer (nighttime temperatures should not be below 55°F). Warm up the soil by using plastic mulch, a cloche, or a cold frame. Space plants 18 in. apart.

GROW In full sun, in a warm, sheltered location. Peppers grow best in fertile, well-drained soil. Amend with compost, lime, and a complete organic fertilizer three weeks prior to planting.

HARVEST Harvest at any stage or size, although fruit is often sweeter after it has turned red (or purple or orange).

ADVICE Hot peppers can be dried for storage. Harvest them when they are ripe, and place them in a 200°F oven for several hours until they are dry and brittle.

IN CONTAINERS Great in containers at least 10 in. deep.

PROBLEMS Aphids, mosaic virus.

POPULAR SELECTIONS Sweet: 'California Wonder 300' is a standard bell pepper that changes from green to red; 'Purple Beauty' produces plenty of dark purple peppers. Hot: try a selection of open-pollinated peppers such as poblano, jalapeno, habanero, serrano, or Hungarian wax.

Poblano peppers can be eaten raw when green and mild, or dried when red for ancho chiles.

PLUM

Prunus domestica
Deciduous tree, hardy in zones 4–10

Plums make a lovely, colorful specimen tree for the small garden. Their foliage can be green, purple, or bronze; their fruit yellow, red, purple, or green; and their blossoms varying shades of pink and white. Easy to grow and widely adapted to many climates, many plum trees are self-pollinating.

START Bare-root or container-grown trees can be transplanted from fall through spring. Spring is better in climates with cold winters; in areas with mild winters, trees can be planted in the fall.

GROW In full sun, in a warm location sheltered from early spring frosts (which can destroy the blossoms). Soil should be rich and well drained. Prune after flowering to maintain shape and size. Plums can be espaliered against a sunny wall. Thin the fruits of Japanese plums when they are very small, leaving 4 to 8 in. between fruits.

HARVEST From early to late summer, depending on type. Ripe plums will be deeply colored and slightly soft; they should come off the branch with a gentle twist.

ADVICE European, Japanese, and American hybrids are available. American hybrids are the most hardy (to –40°F). They are not self-pollinating. European plums are the most widely grown and are hardy; they perform well in all areas except those with very mild winters. Japanese plums are the least hardy and are the best choice for climates with mild winters.

IN CONTAINERS Choose a dwarfing tree and a large container or half-barrel at least 20 in. deep.

PROBLEMS Aphids, bacterial canker, brown rot, caterpillars, plum curculio.

POPULAR SELECTIONS American hybrids: 'Patterson's Pride' is a late-season producer of golden red plums; 'Pembina' produces large, sweet fruit. European: 'Green Gage' produces sweet, yellow-green fruit; the Italian prune plum is a late-season producer of deep-purple fruits with yellow flesh. Japanese: 'Superior' produces round, red fruit; 'Santa Rosa' is an early producer of yellow-fleshed, red-skinned plums.

POTATO

Solanum tuberosum
Cool-season tuber grown as an annual

Although you might not think of potatoes as a worthy small-space crop, they can be grown successfully in tall containers. They are also easy and fun to grow.

START Potatoes are grown by planting seed potatoes—essentially small potatoes. Buy certified disease-free seed potatoes from a seed supplier, or try your luck with farmers' market potatoes. Do not use spuds from the supermarket: they have likely been sprayed with a chemical to prevent sprouting. Chitting your seed potatoes—setting them in a light place to encourage sprouting—can help produce an earlier crop. After they have sprouted, cut larger potatoes into chunks, maintaining at least two "eyes," or sprouts, per piece. Set the pieces on dry newspaper in a bright place for a few days prior to planting to prevent rot. In early spring or midspring, set the seed potatoes 12 in. apart, buried 3 to 4 in. deep with the sprouts facing upward. You can space the plants closer if you prefer smaller potatoes.

GROW In full sun, in rich, well-drained soil high in organic matter. Amend soil with manure and compost prior to planting. Do not add lime. Potatoes prefer a slightly

Potato harvest is a foodie treasure hunt.

Potato, *continued*

acidic soil; mix in coffee grounds, sulfur, or pine needles if your soil is neutral or alkaline. As the plants grow, hill up (add) soil around the plants, leaving the top few inches of plant tips showing. Continue to add soil as the plants grow; potatoes will keep developing along the stalk as the plant grows upward.

HARVEST You can harvest new or baby potatoes after the plant begins to flower. Mature potatoes can be harvested after the foliage begins to die. Potatoes you intend to store should be left in the ground for a week or two after the vines have been removed. Container-grown plants are easily harvested by tipping the container onto a tarp.

ADVICE Potatoes prefer loose, well-cultivated soil, but they will also break up soil as they grow. If your soil isn't loose, you may not get a bumper crop, but the potatoes will help loosen it for next year.

IN CONTAINERS Potatoes do well in large, tall containers such as garbage cans (drill plenty of holes in them for good air circulation). Grow bags are also a good option.

PROBLEMS Blight, Colorado potato beetle, wireworms.

POPULAR SELECTIONS Early season: 'Yukon Gold' is a classic; Midseason: 'All Blue' has blue flesh; 'Kennebec' is a good all-purpose potato. Late season: 'Rose Finn Apple' is a rose-colored fingerling; 'Bintje' is a waxy yellow cultivar.

SUITED TO SMALL SPACES

Among early-season varieties, I'm partial to thin-skinned 'Sieglinde'. The late-season fingerling variety 'Russian Banana' has incredible flavor.

PUMPKIN

see Squash

RADISH

Raphanus sativus
Half-hardy, cool-season annual

One of the quickest crops to mature, radishes are a good choice for beginners, children, and impatient gardeners. Their speediness makes them a great crop for planting alongside slower-growing edibles. In addition to growing the familiar short-season round or mini carrot–shaped salad types, you can also grow slower-maturing Spanish and daikon radishes.

START Direct sow in early spring, succession sowing every one to two weeks until the summer heat hits; then sow again in late summer through fall. Radishes tolerate light frosts, so you can harvest them well into the fall or winter in some climates. Spanish and daikon radishes can be sowed in midsummer to late summer for fall and winter harvests. Space short-season radishes 1 in. apart, and long-season radishes 6 to 8 in. apart.

GROW In full or part sun, in moist, well-drained soil rich in organic matter. The longer-rooted radishes need loose, well-dug soil to develop their roots. Keep the soil moist; radishes become woody if the soil is too dry.

HARVEST Harvest radishes frequently, starting with the thinnings, which can be eaten root, leaves, and all. Radishes are best eaten young; if they remain in the soil too long, they turn woody and overly hot.

ADVICE If your radishes produce seedpods, eat them! Harvest the pods when they are still young and tender, and add them to stir-fries.

IN CONTAINERS Short-season round radishes do well in containers at least 6 in. deep. Longer-rooted radishes require containers 12 in. or deeper.

PROBLEMS Cabbage maggot, clubroot, cutworms, mildew, slugs.

POPULAR SELECTIONS Short-season: 'Easter Egg' is a blend of white, red, purple, and pink radishes, making for a colorful salad; 'White Icicle' looks like a white carrot. Long-season: heirloom 'Black Spanish Round' has a black exterior and is very cold tolerant; 'Summer Cross No. 3' is a daikon type with extra-long roots.

SUITED TO SMALL SPACES

Oblong and red with white tips, 'French Breakfast' is a short-season heirloom.

My daughter loves the surprise of colorful harvests, such as radishes.

RASPBERRY

Rubus idaeus
Perennial cane fruit, hardy in zones 4–10

Similar to blackberries in habit and cultural requirements, raspberries grow best in areas with mild summers. Like blackberries, they are a thicket-forming cane fruit that can be restrained against a wall or fence. Two types of raspberry are common: a summer-bearing type that produces fruit on second-year canes during summer, and an ever-bearing type that produces fruit on year-old canes in fall, followed the next year by a summer crop on second-year canes.

START Bare-root or container-grown plants can be transplanted in early spring. Space plants 2 to 3 ft. apart.

GROW In full or part sun. Soil should be rich in organic matter, moist, and well drained. Plant against a trellis, fence, or wire support, and cut the canes back to 6 in. tall. Tie up new fruit-bearing canes as they grow. After harvest, cut canes that produced fruit that summer back to the ground, leaving the newer canes to produce fruit that fall (for ever-bearers) or next year (for summer bearers).

HARVEST From early summer to fall, depending on type.

ADVICE Raspberries produce suckers; dig up any new canes that may sprout up outside their designated area. Plant at least one summer-bearing and one ever-bearing raspberry to maximize your harvest.

IN CONTAINERS Choose a large container at least 14 in. deep.

PROBLEMS Powdery mildew, verticillium wilt.

POPULAR SELECTIONS Summer-bearing: 'Boyne' is an extremely cold-hardy, early-bearing cultivar with dark,

Raspberry, *continued*

flavorful berries; 'Meeker' is a hardy, productive cultivar with sweet, red fruit. Ever-bearing: 'Fall Gold' produces medium-sized, flavorful yellow berries; bababerry is a red berry suited to areas with mild winters. My favorite variety is the kind you can acquire from a gardening friend or neighbor; raspberries' suckering nature makes them easy to divide.

RHUBARB

Rheum rhabarbarum
Perennial, hardy in zones 2–8

The ultimate in easy-care edibles, rhubarb is a bold, attractive plant that looks at home in an ornamental garden or in a veggie patch. It is not a small plant, but if you can find room for it, it will provide you with delectable, early-spring fruit—or technically, vegetables—for years.

START Rhubarb can be started from seed, but most gardeners start with a nursery-grown plant. Plant late winter to early spring.

GROW In part to full sun, in moist, well-drained soil that is rich in organic matter. Mulch annually with compost or manure. You can force rhubarb to produce earlier growth by covering the dormant plant with an overturned bucket in winter. Cut back any flowering stalks to prolong the harvest.

HARVEST Do not harvest the stalks in the first year. Thereafter, harvest no more than half the stalks in a single year, removing outer stalks at the base of the plant with a firm twist. The earlier stalks are sweeter; by midsummer, they become tough and bitter. The leaves should never be eaten: they are poisonous.

ADVICE Divide plants every third or fourth year to keep them productive.

IN CONTAINERS Choose a large container at least 14 in. deep.

PROBLEMS Rhubarb is fairly free of problems.

POPULAR SELECTIONS 'Victoria' is a sweet, green-and-pink–stemmed cultivar; 'Crimson Cherry' is deep red with a full, rich flavor.

ROSEMARY

Rosmarinus officinalis
Woody evergreen perennial herb, hardy in zones 5–11

In climates with mild winters, rosemary grows outdoors year-round and can develop into a substantial shrub. In colder areas, it can be grown in a container and overwintered indoors. Rosemary takes well to pruning and can be trained as a standard or trimmed as a hedge.

START Purchase nursery-grown plants or take cuttings from another plant in early spring.

GROW In full sun, in exceedingly well-drained soil. Rosemary tolerates part shade and poor soil, as long as the soil isn't soggy. Avoid overwatering; rosemary can succumb to root rot in boggy soils. Pinch back tips to encourage bushy growth.

HARVEST Leaves or sprigs can be harvested as required.

ADVICE Watch for powdery mildew when overwintering rosemary indoors.

IN CONTAINERS Choose containers 8 in. deep.

PROBLEMS Powdery mildew, rot.

POPULAR SELECTIONS 'Arp' is considered the hardiest rosemary, withstanding temperatures of −9°F. 'Golden Rain' is compact and suited to container growing; its foliage is yellow, darkening to green. 'Miss Jessup's Upright' is a tall, narrow cultivar favored by chefs.

Fertilize container-grown rosemary with liquid fish or kelp in spring.

RUTABAGA

Brassica napus

Half-hardy, cool-season biennial, grown as an annual

Rutabaga, also known as winter turnip or swede, is a large, yellow, root vegetable that originated as a cross between the cabbage and the turnip. Because it is frost tolerant and stores well, it is a popular crop for the winter garden.

START Direct sow in midsummer, thinning to 8 in. apart. Keep the soil moist while the seeds are germinating.

GROW In full or part sun, in moist, rich, well-drained soil. Amend with compost, manure, or complete organic fertilizer prior to planting.

HARVEST In areas with cold winters, harvest plump roots in the fall. Light frosts will sweeten the taste. In areas with mild winters, leave the roots in the ground, harvesting as needed.

ADVICE Beyond its familiar role in stews, rutabaga can be eaten raw.

IN CONTAINERS Choose containers at least 12 in. deep.

PROBLEMS Cabbage maggot, clubroot, cutworms, flea beetles, mildew.

POPULAR SELECTIONS 'Laurentian' has purple tops and yellow flesh.

SAGE

Salvia officinalis
Woody perennial herb, hardy in zones 5–11

This hardy evergreen herb is often used in borders, beds, and container groupings for its gray-green, chartreuse, or dusky purple foliage and mauve or blue flowers.

START Transplant nursery-grown plants or root cuttings from another plant in spring, or directly sow seeds in early spring. Space plants 12 in. apart.

Prune sage after flowering to maintain an attractive shape.

GROW In full sun, in well-drained soil. Tolerates part shade and poor soil as long as it isn't soggy. Avoid over-watering. Pinch back tips to encourage bushy growth.

HARVEST Pinch out the tips of the stems or snip whole stems back to soil level. Sage is easily dried for later use.

ADVICE Sage becomes woody and leggy after its third or fourth year and may need replacing; take a cutting and start a new plant.

IN CONTAINERS Choose containers 8 in. deep.

PROBLEMS Powdery mildew, root rot.

POPULAR SELECTIONS Common sage, *Salvia officinalis*, is the best for use as a seasoning; 'Aurea' is compact, with chartreuse foliage and purple blooms; 'Purpurascens' has deep purple foliage. Silver sage, *S. argentea*, has fuzzy silver leaves.

SUITED TO SMALL SPACES

With its variegated, green, white, and purple leaves, 'Tricolor' adds interest to compact gardens.

SOYBEAN

see Bean

SPINACH

Spinacia oleracea
Hardy, cool-season annual

Like radishes, lettuce, and other cool-season crops, spinach tastes best when it is grown and harvested quickly. Spinach bolts in hot weather, but it is a good crop for fall and winter harvests.

START Direct sow six to eight weeks prior to the last frost, succession sowing every two to three weeks until the weather warms. Thin plants to 2 to 3 in. apart. Sow again in late summer for fall and winter harvests.

GROW In full sun or part shade, in a cool location. Soil should be rich, moist, and well drained. Amend with compost, manure, or a complete organic fertilizer prior to planting.

HARVEST Pick a few leaves as needed or snip off the entire plant just above soil level. Leaves are tastiest when young, so harvest them early and often.

ADVICE Although spinach is often difficult to grow in summer, New Zealand spinach (*Tetragonia tetragonioides*) and Malabar spinach (*Basella alba*) both tolerate heat. They are not true spinaches, but their taste is similar. Both can be sown in late spring or summer, in rich, moist soil. New Zealand spinach prefers shade and is perennial in areas with mild winters. Malabar spinach is a vining plant and can be trained up a trellis.

IN CONTAINERS Choose containers 8 in. deep, and be aware that it takes many plants to produce one big salad.

PROBLEMS Leaf miners, mildew, slugs.

POPULAR SELECTIONS Heirloom 'Bloomsdale' has dark green, crinkled leaves; 'Olympia' is great for fall sowing. New Zealand spinach and Malabar spinach are warm-season spinach substitutes.

SUITED TO SMALL SPACES

I enjoy the long harvest season of bolt-resistant cultivar 'Tyee'.

SQUASH

Cucurbita spp.
Tender, warm-season annual

This large group of plants consists of summer favorites zucchini (courgette) and Patty Pan squash, as well as winter classics pumpkin and acorn squash. This distinction between summer and winter squash mostly applies to how we eat these fruits (yes, technically squash is a fruit). Summer squash is harvested when young and is eaten whole—skins, seeds, and all. Winter squash is harvested later in the season, after its skin has thickened. Because of its tough exterior, winter squash stores well. Summer squash, which is usually grown on a bushy—rather than vining—plant, is more suited to the small garden because of its (relatively) compact nature and incredible yields.

START Direct sow in late spring or sow indoors one to two weeks prior to last frost. Space plants 4 ft. apart. Sowing in raised beds or hills (mounded soil) is popular because it improves drainage.

GROW In full sun, in rich, moist, well-drained soil. Amend soil with compost, manure, or a complete organic fertilizer prior to planting. Keep the plants well watered, but avoid getting water on the leaves, which encourages mildew.

HARVEST Summer squash should be harvested when still small for the best flavor and to encourage more fruit production. Summer squash can usually be harvested with a firm twist. Harvest winter squash when the vines have dried and the skin is hard and cannot be marked with your fingernail. Cut winter squash from the vine with a sharp knife.

ADVICE Rotting baby squashes is a sign of inadequate pollination. Step in and do it yourself; for technique, see Cucumber.

Male squash or pumpkin blossoms are delicious, but use them the same day they're picked.

Squash, *continued*

IN CONTAINERS Summer squashes and bush-type winter squash grow well in a large container such as a half-barrel, as long as you add plenty of fertilizer or manure.

PROBLEMS Cucumber beetles, powdery mildew, squash vine borers.

POPULAR SELECTIONS Summer squash: 'Black Beauty' is a classic dark green zucchini; 'Sunray' is a mildew-resistant yellow zucchini; 'Sunburst' is a scalloped, Patty Pan type; 'Tromboncino' is a vine that produces 3-ft., pale green squash; 'Zephyr' is a straightneck type that is yellow with green tips. Winter squash: 'Baby Blue' hubbard squash has unusual blue skin; 'Delicata' is pale with green stripes; 'Buttercup' is sweet and turban-shaped; 'Lumina' produces ghostly white pumpkins; 'Small Sugar' is a classic round pumpkin that is great for pies.

SUITED TO SMALL SPACES

Summer squash: Container-friendly 'Defender' is compact. Winter squash: 'Table King' acorn squash is also good in containers.

STRAWBERRY

Fragaria spp.
Short-lived perennial, hardy in zones 3–10

Strawberries are the ultimate small-space berry crop and grow happily in window boxes, hanging baskets, and nooks and crannies. June-bearing types produce large berries during a short period of time in late spring or early summer; ever-bearing and day-neutral types produce fewer berries from summer through fall.

START Strawberries can be started from seed but are more often propagated from runners—offshoots from a parent plant—and purchased as potted or bare-root plants. Plant in early spring, spacing plants 12 in. apart.

GROW In full or part sun. Soil should be well drained and slightly acidic. Avoid planting in an area that grew members of the nightshade family within the last four years; these crops can carry verticillium wilt. Pinch out any blossoms that appear during the first year. You won't get berries that year, but the plants will be more productive the next. Trim off any runners that appear, in order to force the plant's energy into fruit production. Remove weeds as they appear; strawberries don't like competition. In very cold climates, layer straw over the plants to protect them during the winter.

HARVEST From spring through fall, depending on type. Pick berries when they are red and fully ripe.

ADVICE In the second or third year, you can start new plants by allowing runners to spread and develop baby plants at their tips. After the roots of the baby plants are fully developed, cut the runner and move the plant, if desired.

IN CONTAINERS Great for containers and hanging baskets at least 6 in. deep. Avoid strawberry pots, which tend to dry out quickly.

PROBLEMS Birds, mites, powdery mildew, slugs, verticillium wilt.

POPULAR SELECTIONS June-bearing: 'Cavendish' is hardy and prolific, with large, sweet berries; 'Totem' is extremely hardy and disease resistant with dark red fruit; 'Earliglow' produces flavorful, disease-resistant berries. Ever-bearing: 'Tristar' is disease resistant and has great flavor; 'Tribute' bears fruit early in the season and continues to produce through fall.

SUITED TO SMALL SPACES

Alpine strawberry, *Fragaria vesca*, produces small berries spring through fall and thrives in partial shade.

SWEET POTATO

Ipomoea batatas
Tender perennial, often grown as a warm-season annual

Sweet potatoes are tropical perennials, although they are most often raised as tender annuals. They need hot weather to thrive but are otherwise easy to grow.

START Purchase certified disease-free slips or rooted cuttings, or grow your own by suspending a sweet potato in a glass of water (supporting it with toothpicks so that only part of the tuber is in the water), and waiting for it to develop shoots. Break off the shoots, or slips, and place them in water to grow roots until they are ready to plant. Set them out in late spring or summer after they have been hardened off, 12 to 18 in. apart.

GROW In full sun. Soil should be loose and well drained, but not overly rich. Water regularly, especially until plants are established.

HARVEST Dig carefully before the first frost, and cure (dry) them in a warm, humid location for five days before storing.

ADVICE Sweet potato production decreases when the temperature falls below 64°F. Gardeners in cooler areas can mulch with black plastic to warm the soil.

IN CONTAINERS Choose a compact plant and a container at least 12 in. deep.

PROBLEMS Flea beetles, leafhoppers, wireworms.

POPULAR SELECTIONS 'Georgia Jet' is a quick-maturing cultivar for areas with short seasons.

SUITED TO SMALL SPACES

'Vardaman' is compact and has attractive foliage.

Sweet potatoes store well. Keep in an open box or paper bag at 60°F for up to one year.

THYME

Thymus spp.
Perennial herb, hardy in zones 4–9

Thyme is a shrubby evergreen herb that is both aromatic and attractive. Its pretty flowers attract beneficial insects.

START Transplant nursery-grown plants in spring, take cuttings from a friend's plant, or direct sow seeds in early spring. Space or thin plants 12 in. apart.

GROW In full sun, in well-drained soil. Tolerates part shade and poor soil as long as it is not soggy. Avoid overwatering. Pinch back tips to encourage bushy growth.

HARVEST Harvest by pinching out the tips of the stems or snipping whole stems at soil level. Thyme can be dried for later use.

ADVICE Trim off flowers to promote new growth; the flowers are also edible.

IN CONTAINERS Containers should be at least 6 in. deep.

PROBLEMS Root rot.

POPULAR SELECTIONS Lemon thyme (*Thymus ×citriodorus*) is a favorite among herb gardeners.

SUITED TO SMALL SPACES

Common thyme, *Thymus vulgaris*, is a small-space garden staple and wonderful seasoning.

TOMATO

Solanum lycopersicum
Tender, warm-season perennial grown as an annual

Homegrown tomatoes taste nothing like the commercially grown crops that can be called tomatoes only in appearance. (I started liking tomatoes only after I tasted one I grew myself.) Tomatoes come in sizes ranging from very small (cherry) to large (beefsteak) and in every shape, size, and color imaginable. Tomatoes are classified as indeterminate (vining or cordon) growers, which grow tall and produce fruit over a long period of time, or determinate (bush) growers, which are shorter, bushy, and produce all their fruit at once.

START Start indoors six to eight weeks prior to last frost, or purchase transplants. After the weather has warmed and, ideally, after your plant has begun to flower, transplant it outside after hardening off. Bury the plant in a deep hole, covering the stem up to the first set of true leaves (remove the seed leaves if they are still present). Roots will develop along the buried stem. Bush tomatoes can be spaced 20 in. apart; vining tomatoes should be spaced at least 24 in. apart. Vining tomatoes require tall supports; set up your stakes at planting time. Bush tomatoes also benefit from some support to keep fruit off the ground.

GROW In full sun, in rich, moist, well-drained soil. Amend soil with compost and a complete organic fertilizer prior to planting. Add lime if the soil is acidic. Water consistently; irregular watering is associated with blossom end rot. Pinch out suckers on vining tomatoes to prevent the plants from becoming overly large at the expense of fruit production. Avoid getting water on the leaves, and, if you live in a rainy climate, consider growing tomatoes under

Tomato, *continued*

an awning, porch, or other shelter to prevent the blight caused by wet foliage.

HARVEST Tomatoes are ready after they come away from the vine easily with a gentle twist. If the first frost is approaching and the fruit is still green, you can harvest it and store it in a paper bag along with an apple or banana to speed ripening.

ADVICE At the end of summer, prune any stems that didn't bear fruit, including flower trusses. They will not have time to ripen before the end of summer, so cut them off and force the plant to put its energy into ripening existing fruits.

IN CONTAINERS Bush (determinate) types are better suited for standard containers. Choose one at least 8 in. deep. Indeterminate types need more space: select a half-barrel or other large container.

PROBLEMS Blights, blossom end rot, flea beetles, fusarium wilt, mosaic virus, nematodes, verticillium wilt.

POPULAR SELECTIONS No single tomato variety does well in every climate. Talk to a local nursery and your gardening neighbors for suggestions. Hundreds of selections are available—try something new every year! 'Gardener's Delight' produces large, sweet cherry tomatoes on a vining plant; 'Stupice' is an early-season, bush cultivar that is suited to containers; 'Moneymaker' and 'Mortgage Lifter' are main-season heirloom vining cultivars; 'Brandywine' is a vining, heirloom beefsteak that comes in a variety of colors including pink and black; 'Amish Paste' is an heirloom, vining Roma type that is great for sauces.

SUITED TO SMALL SPACES

'Sungold' is an orange cherry type with incredible flavor; 'Tumbler' is a hybrid bush tomato bred for hanging baskets.

◀ This ingenious planter-in-a-deck supplies a steady crop of tomatoes.

TURNIP

Brassica rapa
Half-hardy, cool-season annual

Turnips are small, white-fleshed root vegetables that are grown similarly to radishes. You can also harvest and eat the young green tops.

START Direct sow in spring, succession sowing every two to three weeks until late summer for a continuous harvest. Turnips tolerate light frosts, so you can harvest them well into the fall or winter in some climates. Thin to 4 to 6 in. apart.

GROW In full sun, in moist, well-drained soil rich in organic matter.

HARVEST Harvest turnips frequently, starting when they are just 1 to 2 in. in diameter. Like radishes, they are best eaten young. Harvest and eat the green tops starting when they are 2 in. tall, pinching off a few from each root.

ADVICE If you are growing turnips mainly for the greens, you can sow seeds closer together and cut back the greens more frequently and thoroughly. Just be aware that the roots will not develop well.

IN CONTAINERS If harvested when small, turnips can get by in a container that is 6 in. deep. Choose a larger container if you plan to let the roots grow large.

PROBLEMS Cabbage maggot, clubroot, flea beetles.

POPULAR SELECTIONS 'Purple Top White Globe' is a classic purple-and-white turnip; 'Golden Globe' has yellow flesh; 'Seven Top' is an heirloom grown for its greens—it does not grow a root.

ZUCCHINI

see Squash

Acknowledgments

This book would never have been written without the love and support of my husband, Ben.

I am also eternally grateful to my parents, Bill and Sandi Bellamy. In addition to introducing me to the pleasures of gardening and good food, they were instrumental in giving me the time and support I needed to write. Thank you.

I would also like to give a big shout out to HeavyPetal.ca readers for their encouragement and enthusiasm. I love the cross-pollination of ideas we've got going!

Thanks are also due to Caitlin and Owen Black, Carole Christopher, City Farmer—Vancouver Compost Demonstration Garden, Matt Kilburn, Lorey Lasley, Pat Logie, the Society Promoting Environmental Conservation, UBC Farm, and Nancy Zbik for letting us photograph their beautiful gardens. Special thanks to Caitlin Black at Aloe Designs, Bill Chalmers at Western Biologicals, Rin at the Farmhouse Farm, and Maninder Tennessey at Atlas Pots for sharing your time and expertise. And thanks to my friends for just being there.

Thanks to the gang at Timber Press, especially Juree Sondker.

And, finally, I'd like to thank worms for doing so much of the grunt work. You guys rock.

Bibliography

Ashworth, Suzanne. 2002. *Seed to Seed: Seed Saving and Growing Techniques for Vegetable Gardeners.* Decorah, Iowa: Seed Savers Exchange.

Beck, Alison. 2008. *The Canadian Edible Garden: Vegetables, Herbs, Fruits & Seeds.* Edmonton, Alberta: Lone Pine.

Beck, Alison, and Louise Donnelly. 2009. *Fruit and Berry Gardening for Canada.* Edmonton, Alberta: Lone Pine.

Cunningham, Sally Jean. 2000. *Great Garden Companions: A Companion-Planting System for a Beautiful, Chemical-Free Vegetable Garden.* Emmaus, Pennsylvania: Rodale Press.

Ellis, Barbara W., and Fern Marshall Bradley, eds. 1996. *The Organic Gardener's Handbook of Natural Insect and Disease Control: A Complete Problem-Solving Guide to Keeping Your Garden & Yard Healthy Without Chemicals.* Emmaus, Pennsylvania: Rodale Press.

Environmental Working Group. 2010. "Shoppers Guide to Pesticides." http://www.foodnews.org/walletguide.php. Accessed 14 July 2010.

Fowler, Alys. 2008. *Garden Anywhere: How to Grow Gorgeous Container Gardens, Herb Gardens, Kitchen Gardens, and More—Without Spending a Fortune.* San Francisco: Chronicle Books, LLC.

Gillman, Jeff. 2008. *The Truth About Garden Remedies: What Works, What Doesn't, and Why.* Portland, Oregon: Timber Press.

———. 2008. *The Truth About Organic Gardening: Benefits, Drawbacks, and the Bottom Line.* Portland, Oregon: Timber Press.

Guerra, Michael. 2000. *The Edible Container Garden: Growing Fresh Food in Small Spaces.* New York: Fireside/Simon & Schuster.

Herriot, Carolyn. 2005. *A Year on the Garden Path: A 52-Week Organic Gardening Guide.* Victoria, British Columbia: Earthfuture Publications.

Logsdon, Gene. 2009. *Small-Scale Grain Raising: An Organic Guide to Growing, Processing, and Using Nutritious Whole Grains, for Home Gardeners and Local Farmers.* 2d ed. White River Junction, Vermont: Chelsea Green Publishing.

Reynolds, Richard. 2009. *On Guerilla Gardening: A Handbook for Gardening Without Boundaries.* London: Bloomsbury UK.

Solomon, Steve. 2006. *Gardening When It Counts: Growing Food in Hard Times.* Gabriola Island, British Columbia: New Society Publishers.

Stamets, Paul. 2000. *Growing Gourmet and Medicinal Mushrooms.* Berkeley, California: Ten Speed Press.

Trail, Gayla. 2005. *You Grow Girl: The Groundbreaking Guide to Gardening.* New York, New York: Fireside/Simon & Schuster.

West Coast Seeds. 2009 *West Coast Seeds Catalogue.* Vancouver, Canada.

White, Hazel, Janet H. Sanchez, and the editors of Sunset Books. 2005. *The Edible Garden.* Menlo Park, California: Sunset Publishing Corporation.

Metric Conversions

INCHES	CENTIMETERS
¼	0.6
½	1.3
¾	1.9
1	2.5
2	5.1
3	7.6
4	10
5	13
6	15
7	18
8	20
9	23
10	25
20	51
30	76
40	100
50	130
60	150
70	180
80	200
90	230
100	250

FEET	METERS
1	0.3
2	0.6
3	0.9
4	1.2
5	1.5
6	1.8
7	2.1
8	2.4
9	2.7
10	3
20	6
30	9
40	12
50	15
60	18
70	21
80	24
90	27
100	30

TEMPERATURES

$$°C = \tfrac{5}{9} \times (°F - 32)$$

$$°F = (\tfrac{9}{5} \times °C) + 32$$

Photography Credits

Alamy Nigel Cattlin: 119; Alex Hinds: 66

Andrea Bellamy 11, 21 top, 65 upper left and right, lower left, 77, 115 lower left, 134 lower left, 173, 191

Bugwood.org Joseph Berger: 116 lower left; Gary Bernon, USDA APHIS: 117 upper left; L.L. Berry: p. 114 upper right; William M. Brown Jr. 122 lower left; Eric Coombs, Oregon Department of Agriculture: 122 upper right; Clemson University—USDA Cooperative Extension Slide Series: 116 lower right, 117 lower right, 121 upper left, 122 lower right; Whitney Cranshaw, Colorado State University: 111, 112 upper left, lower left, 113 upper left and right, lower right, 114 upper left; John C. French, Sr., Retired, Universities: Auburn, GA, Clemson and U of MO: 113 lower left; Jonas Janner Hamann: Universidade Federal de Santa Maria: 120 upper left; Gerald Holmes, Valent USA Corporation: 116 upper right, 117 upper right, 119 upper right, 123; A.C. Magyarosy: 115 upper left; Oliver T. Neher, The Amalgamated Sugar Company: 120 upper right; Frank Peairs, Colorado State University: 114 lower left, 115 lower right, 118 lower right, 121 upper left, 122 lower right; O.P. Sharma: 116 upper left; Howard F. Schwartz, Colorado State University: 122 upper left; USDA ARS Photo Unit, USDA Agricultural Research Service: 115 upper right; University of Georgia Plant Pathology Archive, University of Georgia: 121 upper right

GAP Photos Elke Borkowski: 2; Keith Burdett: 145; Sarah Cuttle: 105; Heather Edwards: 6; Victoria Firmston: 82; Michael King: 22; Clive Nichols: 200; Gary Smith: 80; Friedrich Strauss: 12, 23, 42, 92, 94, 130

James Dill, University of Maine Cooperative Extension: 112 lower right

Lindsey J. duToit 120 lower left

Garden Collection FLPA/Gary K. Smith: 136; Derek St. Romaine: 54, 111, 126; Neil Sutherland: 33

Ben Garfinkel 65 lower right, 187

Saxon Holt 37

iStockphoto akit: 175; bedo: 159; CreativeFire: 194; dancingfishes: 138; dianazh: 193; Dleonis: 171; dmitrii_designer: 133; hbak: 44 left, 163; iDymax: 70; jklune: 14; kcline: 50; Lehner: 61; Lokibaho: 57; Mannisen: 48; Marbury: 189; motorolka: 176; NikonShutterman: 180; PauuletHohn: 144; Peter_Nile: 44 right; PrairieArtProject: 71; Ratikova: 185; redmal: 104; SharonFoelz: 40; Sisoje: 46; SkyF: 166; smartstock: 198; SondraP: 167; stocknshares: 149; StockSolutions: 132; Ulga: 73; Woolfenden: 182; wyndy25: 184; xeni4ka: 151; Youngvet: 15

Steve Masley Front cover lower right, 8, 30

Mario Mirelez 49

Susy Morris 88

Peterson Garden Project 13

Shutterstock Elena Elisseeva: 21; Natalia Evstigneeva: 110; Nemeziya: 112 upper right; ninikas: 142; Shevs: 59; smereka: 129

Verdura Gardens 16, 26, 27, 62, 63, 101, 128

All other photos by Jackie Connelly

Index

About the Author

Andrea Bellamy is the creator of *Heavy Petal* (heavypetal. ca), a blog devoted to urban organic gardening. She has a certificate in garden design from the University of British Columbia and studied permaculture methods for food production at an urban microfarm. She has been gardening since childhood and has grown food on rooftops, balconies, boulevards, and patios, and in community garden beds, window boxes, traffic circles, front yards, and backyards. She is the Edible Gardens columnist for *Edible Vancouver* magazine, for which she won a Silver Award of Achievement from the Garden Writers Association. Her writing has appeared in a number of online and print publications. She lives in Vancouver, Canada, with her husband and daughter.